When You Think about It

When You Think about It

Ten Lessons from Philosophical Skepticism

Robert C. Robinson

CASCADE *Books* · Eugene, Oregon

WHEN YOU THINK ABOUT IT
Ten Lessons from Philosophical Skepticism

Copyright © 2024 Robert C. Robinson. All rights reserved. Except for brief quotations in critical publications or reviews, no part of this book may be reproduced in any manner without prior written permission from the publisher. Write: Permissions, Wipf and Stock Publishers, 199 W. 8th Ave., Suite 3, Eugene, OR 97401.

Cascade Books
An Imprint of Wipf and Stock Publishers
199 W. 8th Ave., Suite 3
Eugene, OR 97401

www.wipfandstock.com

PAPERBACK ISBN: 978-1-6667-0174-6
HARDCOVER ISBN: 978-1-6667-0175-3
EBOOK ISBN: 978-1-6667-0176-0

Cataloguing-in-Publication data:

Names: Robinson, Robert C., author.

Title: When you think about it : ten lessons from philosophical skepticism / Robert C. Robinson.

Description: Eugene, OR : Cascade Books, 2024 | Includes bibliographical references and index.

Identifiers: ISBN 978-1-6667-0174-6 (paperback) | ISBN 978-1-6667-0175-3 (hardcover) | ISBN 978-1-6667-0176-0 (ebook)

Subjects: LCSH: Philosophy. | Skepticism.

Classification: B74 .R63 2024 (print) | B74 .R63 (ebook)

05/09/24

This book is dedicated to
Janeann Connor
My Grandmother

Philosophy Begins in Wonder.
—PLATO'S SOCRATES, *THEAETETUS* 155C-D

Contents

Acknowledgments | ix

1. Introduction | 1
2. Descartes, Doubt, and Skepticism | 10
3. Hume and the Problem of Induction | 17
4. The Euthyphro Dilemma | 26
5. Egoism, Relativism, and Moral Philosophy | 33
6. The Ontological Argument for the Existence of God | 47
7. The Teleological Argument for the Existence of God | 56
8. Berkeley's Idealist Argument Against the Existence of the Material World | 65
9. Social Contract Theory | 78
10. Artificial Intelligence | 88
11. Paradoxes | 98

Bibliography | 107
Index | 109

Acknowledgments

I WOULD LIKE TO thank Amy Invernizzi and Andrew Beck, along with four anonymous reviewers, for invaluable feedback and advice on very early drafts of the manuscript. Thanks to George Callihan, Charlie Collier, my editor, and the staff at Wipf and Stock for turning my messy manuscript into the completed book you hold in your hand (as always, any remaining errors or omissions are no one's fault but my own).

Thank you to my students; discussing these topics over the years has strengthened my own understanding of them, and I hope that you've been able to take away something valuable, too! Of course, I also owe an earlier debt of gratitude to my own teachers. Thank you to Alex Kaufman who patiently taught me so much, and to Audrey Haynes, who saw my potential early on.

Thanks to my grandmother, Janeann Connor, to whom this book is dedicated. Every time I hand her a book, she asks when the next one will be finished. Thanks for keeping me writing, Grandma.

Thanks to Anlys Olivera for supporting me in whatever I do.

CHAPTER 1

Introduction

WHAT IS PHILOSOPHY? WHAT do philosophers do? What makes one action or question philosophical, and another one not? How does one philosophize? Philosophy is sometimes a difficult subject to define in a precise way. That is, there is understandable disagreement about what makes a topic philosophical, and what exactly we mean by philosophy. However, I'll try to explain what is included in philosophy, and which things probably shouldn't be, in an effort to try to circle around and narrow down what we mean by the term.

I take it that philosophy is dedicated to answering big, hard questions, but of course that does not denote the entire domain of philosophy. Questions in pure mathematics are certainly hard, though it's not clear that they're philosophical questions (though maybe some are). And hardly any questions are bigger than those neatly in the domain of astrophysics—they are questions about the biggest things we know about, after all—and questions about stars and planets and space are probably mostly outside the domain of philosophers.

Nonetheless, big, hard problems are those typically that interest philosophers. We may further limit the list of problems to those that, for the most part, cannot be solved empirically. Interestingly, most of the domains we typically think of as the hard sciences, such as biology, astronomy, or physics, along with most of the social sciences, such as economics, psychology, or politics, have their start in the history of philosophy. Aristotle was a biologist, and while many of his predecessors theorized about the mechanisms of life, Aristotle cut open animals and systematically analyzed and documented the goings on in the animals' interior lives. Before there was a department of psychology on any college campus, disagreements and dialogues between luminary philosophers such as Locke, Berkeley, and Hume formed the foundations of investigations into the mysteries of consciousness, minds, and ideas. Adam Smith, Karl Marx, and John Stuart Mill wrote some of the original investigations into production, distribution, and consumption, which would form the foundation of economics. And for as long as there have been people, there have been people sitting in the grass at night, staring into the sky, wondering what was up there.

Early scientific investigations were known as natural philosophy, though as theoretical tools come to be replaced with empirical ones, those areas of investigation begin to move into their own domains and subsequently get their own departments in colleges and universities. People got tired of speculating about what those lights are in the sky at night, until someone finally invented a telescope, which allowed them to begin to look more closely and find out for sure. With the development of those empirical tools, the question stopped being a philosophical one and started to inhabit its own area of science. Likewise, empirical tools allow psychologists to make more formal investigations into the parts and operation of the brain. Statistical methods and computer models helped create political scientists who can test questions about human behavior and politics, and the scientific method helped to systematize the investigation into economic theories, allowing for more empirical tests, and granting greater predictive power.

There are, however, a number of big, hard questions remaining, and many of those are typically still reserved for philosophers. We ask questions in metaphysics, including what exists, and what kinds of things do or can exist; we ask questions in epistemology, including what we can know, and how we can know that we know what we know. Philosophy of religion (which is separate from the *practice* of religion) allows for questions about the nature and/or existence of God, or other supernatural creatures. Aesthetics is the investigation into art and beauty. Moral and political philosophy ask questions about how we should treat each other, what can be said about goodness at all, and what are the best ways to organize our societies as systems of mutual cooperation. Who knows—someday someone may invent an instrument that will let us look at the nature of justice in an empirical way just like the telescope allowed astronomers and early philosophers to empirically observe the heavens. Until then, philosophers will continue to think about these matters.

While it is difficult to denote the specific contours of philosophy, a few things can be said to try to contain what we mean by it. First, as I describe above, philosophical problems are big, and by that I mean that they are complex, in that they have many facets, and that looking at any one of them reveals many more. Take, for example, the issue of the use of capital punishment as a response to the most heinous crimes. Critics may disagree on the legitimate use of capital punishment, for example whether its existence does in fact deter future crimes. But assuming it does, another question arises about whether we feel justified in using a person's death in order to achieve some public policy. Even if, for example, deterrence is the goal, we may still debate whether or not it matters that sometimes innocent people are executed, so long as the existence of capital punishment has a deterrent effect. The first is an empirical question, but its answer still leaves open the second, normative question.

At the same time, critics may argue that capital punishment is a required response to our political commitments that a person should receive what is owed to him, and a person who commits the worst kinds of crimes deserves the harshest punishment. Looking more closely, however, we might disagree about which punishment is the harshest (a life spent in prison without the possibility of release might be considered worse than a quick death). And other questions present themselves: does torture satisfy the demands of retributive justice? If so, should we do it? If retributive justice is based on the assumption that what a person deserves is based on what he freely does, will our intuitions change if the criminal's choices were limited by social or economic circumstances or mental health problems? Does free will even exist?

This leads to a second contour of philosophy, and that is while in many cases solutions to, or explanations of, philosophical problems may rely on empirical evidence or facts, it does not *only* rely on them. That is, philosophical problems are never resolved by mere appeal to facts. Take again the question about the legitimacy of the use of capital punishment for the worst crimes. One of the fundamental issues here is a forward-looking one, namely whether keeping the death penalty deters some would-be murderers from committing their crime. This is an empirical question, resolvable perhaps through psychological analysis of criminals, polls or surveys of people who commit crimes but fall short of murder, and even our anecdotal intuitions—would the knowledge that you may face execution dissuade you from murder? However, the philosophical question is not resolved here. In some situations, given the same crime of murder, extenuating circumstances lead a jury to decide that one case deserves a harsher punishment than another (due perhaps to premeditation, mental illness, past history of abuse, etc.). When we look even deeper, as we noted, we find an ethical question about the legitimacy of using a person and his death to forward a policy goal. Do we have the right to use people in that way?

A third contour arises out of these ideas. And that is, again, while a philosophical problem may rely on facts (and it does not always, as we will see below in some more abstract cases in metaphysics), it is at core a conceptual problem. I'll discuss the philosophical methodology of *conceptual analysis* below, but for now this is a sufficiently important point and worth pondering for a moment.

Suppose the question is, "How many bricks were used to create the facade of the Empire State Building?" Given the question, the answer will be straightforward, and factual, and will consist in the end in some particular (though fantastically large) number. One could go about trying to find that answer in any number of ways. You might hang a scaffold from the top and, notebook in hand, count the bricks as you slowly descend to street level. Or you might measure a small part of the building, say the number of bricks in the first story, and then estimate, based on the fact that the building is 102 stories tall. Or you might bribe a clerk at the architectural firm who designed it to give you the plans and original blueprint. And let us speculate that each of the three methods would ultimately arrive at a different sum. The key take-away here is that the issue is resolved by consideration of the facts. There may be disagreement based on the methods employed, but there is no deep, remaining conceptual issue to resolve.

But the same is not true of our example of capital punishment—or indeed any philosophical issue. The philosophical problem is tangled up in the empirical one, but the part of the question that is philosophical, and so the part that is interesting to philosophers, comes down to more complex concepts of, e.g., right and wrong (for example, is it ever justified to use a person merely as a means to an end?) or the problem of desert (for example, does free will exist, or is it only an illusion?). In the first case, we might reason that actions are to be judged to be morally correct merely as a function of how much happiness they cause in the general public. And if that's the case, we should always aim our choices in a way that benefits the intellectual and/or physical pleasures of the greatest number of people. If that's so, then looking at the issue of capital punishment, it is largely irrelevant whether it treats a person as a mere means to an end—individual dignity or autonomy plays no role in the calculation. A competing moral conception might dispute that it is the pleasure as a consequence of action that makes actions and choices right—instead we should ignore the consequences and hold individual dignity as central, perhaps treating all others according to some universal principle that matches the way I also desire to be treated. In this case, as I know that I would not like for my death to be a tool in advancing some political end (particularly if I'm innocent of the crime), then the deterrent argument fails to persuade, even if the facts do support the conclusion that the death penalty deters future crimes.

Deterrence is a forward-looking justification for the death penalty, but there is also a backward-looking justification that requires that retribution be applied to all crimes, and so the worst punishment is reserved and required for the worst crimes. While the principle of "an eye for an eye" is an over-simplification, the intuition that a person should receive a punishment in proportion to the crime is still a compelling one. Here, again, there are certain relevant facts that we may consider. For example, there are legal standards that constrain which punishments are justified; in the West at least, punishments that involve torture or permanent bodily damage violate constitutional or other legal precedent, and so cannot be applied. We might consider psychological, legal, or other factual sciences in determining which punishments are the worst—is a person sufficiently punished with a quick painless death, or do the most heinous crimes recommend a long prison sentence, perhaps with elements of hard labor or deprivation of certain luxuries (e.g., television, food options, reading materials)? These are the empirical questions (i.e., which punishment causes more psychological suffering), but while the philosophical questions are tangled up with the empirical, they themselves are conceptual in nature. The retributive theory of punishment is based on a standard test in common law regarding the mental element, or intention, of a person to commit his crime. This is known in legal scholarship by the Latin *mens rea*, which means "guilty mind"; to be deserving of retributive punishment for an action, your action must be based on a guilty intention to commit the crime. Pushing your older brother down the stairs to collect his share of the inheritance betrays an intention. Accidentally losing your balance and knocking your brother down the stairs, while clumsy and careless, does not betray the same guilty intention, and so the two cases will be treated differently. The latter was simply bad luck. Our moral intuition helps to guide this judgment. In the end, while our judgment does rely on facts, the philosophical problem is at its core a conceptual, not a factual, problem.

A final contour of the domain of philosophy is that philosophical explanations aim to be deep, rather than broad. We've all had that experience of staying up late having a long, serious conversation with a close friend about important, meaningful subjects. Those events are meaningful and memorable because you felt free to dig deeply, putting aside superficial, commonsense explanations, and instead aimed to uncover more fundamental principles. What you were doing was philosophy, and that's what philosophers do all the time. In *The Republic*, Plato tells a parable about a group of men who have spent their lives chained to a bench, deep in a cave.

With a fire burning behind them, what they see are shadows dancing and moving on the wall in front of their faces—their entire reality is what they perceive on the wall. However, when one of the men escapes his chains and leaves the cave, he's able to see the world for what it is—bright sunny skies, tall trees, green grass. Because his eyes have never seen sunlight, the images are painful. And while the images are frightening, the truth of the world is too compelling, so he goes on to explore with great interest.

At the conclusion of the tale, the man returns to the cave to tell others what he has learned, and to explain to them that what they see is mere shadow, or imitation, of reality. Unfortunately, given that their perception of reality is limited entirely to the shadow, they mock and ridicule him, and call him delusional. The man, of course, is the philosopher, who is not satisfied with a superficial representation of the world and so investigates and aims to penetrate common sense and arrive at an understanding of the real and true nature of the world and reality.

Before moving on, there is one more lesson to draw from Plato's Allegory of the Cave: philosophy is dangerous. As you can see, philosophical investigation is absolutely committed to putting aside even deeply held beliefs and holding every idea up to scrutiny. Nothing is sacred or believed or held to be true because others believe it, or because it has always been done that way. Philosophy requires that you follow the truth wherever it leads. When the man returned to the cave, the images and ideas he brought back were frightening to those who were still there. Understandably, it is easier and more comfortable to continue to believe in the things we've always believed, regardless of whether they are true. And so the men threatened him, mocked him, and chased him out of their company. But philosophy is like this. Imagine what may happen in your home life if you discover and take seriously the conclusion that there is no rational basis for a belief in a higher power. Imagine what the world would look like if we find that baked into the fundamental design of a capitalist political economy is the necessary exploitation of the worker, and that there's an alternative economic system that frees people from that exploitation. Who exactly would benefit from this knowledge, and who would be harmed? Think about what happened to Galileo when he discovered evidence that the earth, and God's chosen people on it, were not at the center of the universe (I'll tell you—he was nearly executed for telling people of this discovery). People, and particularly people with power and authority, have a vested interest in maintaining the status quo, regardless of whether the basis on which we hold it is truth or not. Philosophy is a powerful weapon against ignorance and dogmatically held beliefs.

What have we learned so far? Philosophy is not simply whatever you want it to be, and the conclusions of philosophy are not whatever you want them to be. Philosophy is not a discipline for which there are no right or wrong answers. Rather, philosophy is aimed at issues and explanations that are complex, and resolutions and explanations regarding those issues are derived using rigorous argumentative tools. Regardless of whether they also involve appeal to empirical facts, the philosophical elements are those that focus on concepts, not strictly the facts. Philosophical explanations are deep, designed by their nature to go beyond the apparent and superficial. And of course, a commitment to uncovering the actual true nature of things can result in alienation from family and society (though it is hoped that the days of executing people for holding a commitment to uncomfortable facts are behind us).

Don't be fooled, though. That there are a lack of empirical tools does not mean that the field of philosophy is entirely subjective, or that there are no agreed upon, formal methodologies to help answer these questions in a systematic way. Logic is an extremely powerful tool, focused on argumentation and truth preservation. Fundamentally, in an analysis of a concept or idea, we want to be sure that we're starting from positions and foundations that are true, and that any inferences that we make from those foundations avoid a move from a true premise to a false conclusion. A good argument never leads you from good, true reasons, to accept a bad or false conclusion. In the next chapter we'll see what happens when someone (in this case Descartes) is absolutely committed to this principle of beginning from indisputably true premises and relying only on inferences that must preserve truth.

Another tool deployed by the philosopher is known as the Socratic method—so powerful a tool that it is widely employed in any number of domains, and in particular in education, which is where you might have heard of it. This makes sense, since it was developed by Socrates and Plato in order to educate people. The Socratic method works through dialogue: Socrates asks an expert about some concept or definition (such as beauty or goodness or justice), and when a definition is given, he moves the dialogue by thinking of some unnoticed caveat, or counter-example, and gives it back. The dialogue then progresses by refining the concept or definition in the face of these counter-examples. The goal is that by excluding instances or examples that are not included, and keeping those that are, we thus come closer and closer to the true nature of the concept under investigation. A trivial example will help drive the method home.

If I ask you what is an elephant, you may reply that it is a gray animal that is native to parts of Africa and Asia. Showing you a photo of an African mole rat, you could remind me that the elephant is a quite large animal. I could show you a picture of a hippopotamus and ask if this is also an elephant. No, you'd reply, an elephant has large floppy ears and also a trunk for a nose, and so on. Here, you can see the Socratic method in action: I inquire for a definition, you provide one, and I scrutinize it, thinking of counterexamples and, if there are any, giving you an opportunity to revise your definition accordingly. Where you arrive (e.g., a large mammal with floppy ears and a trunk for a nose native to parts of Africa and Asia) is closer to the truth than where we started. And that is the goal of the method—a dialogue in which concepts are revised and refined to exclude instances or examples that do not correspond to the concept, but to include those that do.

The Socratic method is thus closely related to what some philosophers simply call conceptual analysis. When thinking about complex, subtle issues such as beauty, freedom, or justice, it is useful when we carefully consider and analyze the way that we use the concept. In doing so, we may ask hard questions in order to more closely inspect the concept under analysis. For example, if a man is transported, unaware, into a room, and in that room is a person he wants to visit with and talk to, would we say that he stayed voluntarily or freely, even if the doors were locked and he could not leave? On the one hand, it seems that voluntariness requires an ability to do otherwise, so he did not stay freely. On the other hand, voluntariness requires volition or willingness to act, and he stayed in the room of his own volition, so he did stay freely. So which is it?

This question, which I owe to John Locke (from his *Essays Concerning Human Understanding* [1690]), is an example of another tool employed by philosophers, which we call a thought experiment. Thought experiments are extremely valuable tools for analyzing concepts in a logical way, when no other empirical method is available. They're so valuable that they've been employed outside of philosophy, most notably by Galileo who argued persuasively that two objects fall at the same rate, regardless of their mass, and by Einstein, who used a thought experiment to clarify the special theory of relativity. Thought experiments are useful for analyzing difficult or impossible situations, to give an insight into some concept. Notice that Locke didn't actually have to lock anyone in a room, Galileo didn't actually have to drop two objects from the Leaning Tower of Pisa, and Einstein didn't have to accelerate to the speed of light to observe the light wave.

Finally, let me mention the logical argument form sometimes known as *reductio ad absurdum*. This is an argument form that proceeds from the position that if we assume some proposition A, and from that we can derive both sentence X and sentence not-X, then we can conclude that the original proposition A is false. More straightforwardly, if you can derive a contradiction from something, then that something must be false. As an example, take my initial worry, above, that there are no correct answers to problems in philosophy. Now this proposition:

(1) there are no correct answers to problems in philosophy

is either correct or incorrect—either true or false. Now, if it is correct, then you've successfully identified a correct proposition in philosophy—namely (1). So there are correct answers in philosophy (or at least one correct answer, since (1) is one). At the same time, if (1) is not correct—that is, it's false that there are no correct answers to problems in philosophy, then of course it is because philosophy does allow for at least some correct answers. In either case, we've arrived at a paradox of the form both X and not-X, and so we should reject the initial assumption, which was "there are no correct answers to problems in philosophy." Less formally, since from A you can derive some propositions that we would otherwise reject, then we should also reject A. (And of course, another take-away here is that we should be very skeptical of the claim that there are no correct answers to problems in philosophy).

It's useful to begin by thinking about the methodological approach that philosophers undertake for a number of reasons. First, I want to dispel a popular notion that philosophy is a discipline involved in talking about questions that have no answers. It is a fallacy to think that since we don't know the answer, or don't know how we can definitely know the answer, that there is not one. Rather, philosophers generally operate under the assumption that there are right, or at least better, answers to the questions that they ask, and that they have a number of tools to try to come closer and closer to an understanding of these concepts under investigation, and to the answers to those questions. Second, since we'll look closely at some big, surprising arguments from the history of philosophy, one benefits first from a methodological primer. Let's begin!

Works Referenced in This Chapter

Plato (375 BCE/2004). *The Republic.*
Descartes, René (1641/1999). *Discourse on Method and Meditations on First Philosophy.*
Locke, John (1690). *An Essay Concerning Human Understanding.*

Further Suggested Reading

Russell, Bertrand (1912/1997). *The Problems of Philosophy.*
Durant, William (1926). *The Story of Philosophy.*
Blackburn, Simon (1999). *Think: A Compelling Introduction to Philosophy.*

CHAPTER 2

Descartes, Doubt, and Skepticism

IN THIS CHAPTER, I want to ease into an argument, though at the same time continue to think about the methods and approaches of philosophy. In particular, this chapter is about skepticism, which is foundational to philosophical investigation. Philosophers use the term "skepticism" somewhat differently than many people sometimes do in the colloquial sense. Readers are no doubt familiar with so-called "climate skeptics" or "skeptics about the moon landing." These individuals, perhaps through a distrust of the government, popular media, or other figures of authority (real or perceived) reject any evidence for the position outright, and then claim positively that the position is false. Included in this category are many conspiracy theorists who are similarly "skeptical" of evidence whose origins include sources that they distrust.

Philosophical skepticism is different entirely. When we rely on skepticism as a philosophical tool, we do not mean it as in actively believing that some particular proposition is false, but rather as a means to temporarily suspend judgment about the truth of the proposition until more evidence is collected. More charitably, skepticism requires that the extent to which you believe a proposition to be true should vary in proportion to the evidence, and the strength of that evidence, in support of the proposition.

Philosophical skepticism is not specific; that is, it's not aimed at any particular belief or conclusion that we want to call into doubt, as in the examples above. Rather, it is an active, general process, or worldview, aimed outwardly. You can think of it as a kind of epistemic filter, so that before accepting any fact or truth, we've taken the active step to hold it up to sufficient scrutiny. If one deems that the evidence for it is sufficient, then one may, perhaps tentatively, accept it as true. If there are good reasons to call it into doubt, then that is done, subjecting it to further rounds of scrutiny until either accepting (again tentatively) or rejecting the truth of the claim. The philosophical method, as we've seen, does not allow for anything to be taken to be true merely dogmatically, and it does not allow for the acceptance or inference of a claim without sufficient reason.

This activity can be more difficult than it sounds, and so we'll benefit, before moving on to more specific arguments, to think about Descartes, and his method of hyperbolic doubt.

Though the eighteenth century Scottish philosopher David Hume is known as the most formidable of the philosophical skeptics, the method of doubt and skepticism was honed by Descartes much earlier than that. Before the era of modern philosophy, which is loosely correlated with the enlightenment period, philosophy quite often tended to proceed from the assumption of God's influence on this or that and took as its duty to try to understand the mechanism of the influence. The Middle Ages are a good example of this—very little of what was produced during that time is taken seriously by contemporary philosophers, and much of what is left includes either topics that are theological in its nature, or which do take seriously some philosophical topic, but do with an eye toward theological apologism. And so before Descartes's notable *Meditations on First Philosophy*, God's existence and influence was often assumed as true unreflectively and without much argumentation; philosophical insights were subsequently derived from that assumption, or at least in conjunction with an assumption of the handiwork of God.

Figure 1. René Descartes

Descartes suggested that, if we are to know anything for certain, then our knowledge should be grounded on an unshakable foundation. If there is any doubt—any at all—that something may not be absolutely true, then we should, at least for the sake of the argument, discard it in favor of some proposition that is indubitable or impossible to doubt. When Descartes suggested that we should doubt anything not known to be absolutely true, he was indeed speaking hyperbolically. Descartes was a good Catholic and believed in the existence of the Christian God. However, this was excluded since, even though he believed it to be true, it was at least logically possible to call it into doubt. The method of hyperbolic doubt says that we should exclude any proposition that is even remotely, possibly untrue, no matter how readily and earnestly we believe it. If we can find something entirely undoubtable, and then we can build all knowledge on that, then our worldview—our knowledge and beliefs about the world—will be based on an entirely solid foundation.

On the face of it, while this may seem like a fun diversion, it may appear nothing more than a silly philosophical exercise in mental gymnastics. What can be the point of rejecting things that everyone knows to be obviously true, except as a type of mental puzzle? And yet Descartes's argument represents an important historical and philosophical break with the Middle Ages, in which few serious philosophers would have thought to doubt the existence of God, at least not in a serious, public way. Descartes relied on a system in which it is legitimate to call any belief or idea into doubt. He applied a system of skepticism, willed to us by Plato and Aristotle, and in which we are free to suspend judgment about whether a proposition is true, until we've had a chance to evaluate the evidence both in support of it and against it, along with any subsequent propositions or ideas that can be derived from it. It's a rigorous process.

Consider it: what do you know, or can you know, with absolute certainty? Taken seriously, this question is more difficult than it seems. For example, you might submit that you can trust your senses; if you see something, then you know that it's there. But, Descartes replies, are you absolutely sure, every time? Have you ever seen an optical illusion? Have you ever been mistaken by your senses? He describes seeing a tower in the distance that looks cylindrical, but when approached more closely, he discovers that it's actually square shaped. While you are probably right that what you're holding in your hand is a book, if you're honest, you'll admit that there's a tiny chance that you're mistaken. Your senses have deceived you in the past, and so, strictly speaking, it's not impossible that they're doing it right now. And if it's even remotely possible to doubt it, then we call it into doubt, and continue looking elsewhere.

That's the method. What can I know without any doubt, and how can I know it? Think about what you know. Where do people tend to get their information? You believe that the world is a particular way and contains objects of a particular kind, because you've seen them. That is, you've experienced them with your senses. Should we say that what you've seen with your own eyes is something that you know to be true? Not really, since everyone has been mistaken at one time or another in their sensory judgments. Two tracks on a railroad appear to converge in the distance, but when you arrive at that spot, they are still parallel. Heat dissipating from a flat surface such as the highway in the distance gives the impression of water where, when you arrive at the spot, there is none. And so what can we say about the principle by which we should always believe our senses? That principle will sometimes lead us astray. If what we want is to know with absolute certainty, we will need something stronger than reliance on your sensory perceptions.

You might legitimately reply that, while your senses do sometimes deceive you in particular cases about what in particular is there (such as an optical illusion), nonetheless your senses are reliable in that they tell you that *something* is there. That is, if you mistake a square building for a round one in the distance, or are mistaken about a thing's shape because of the refractive elements of water, or heat rising from it, you can nonetheless be certain that something is there. Right? Your senses sometimes get it wrong, but what they get right is that the physical world exists. Right? Is this something that you have enough evidence to know, without any dispute, and with logical certainty? Think about it.

Let me pose a question. Have you ever had a dream that felt so real, that when you awoke, you nearly can't believe that it wasn't? Have you ever had the experience in a dream where someone was mean or cruel, and even after you awake and realize it was a dream, you're still a little bit angry at that person? Alternatively, have you ever been in trouble with a friend or a loved one because of something you did in *their* dream? Dreams can seem very real, and when they're occurring they can be indistinguishable from reality. Here's the question: if it's true that while you are in a dream the experience is sometimes indistinguishable from reality, are you absolutely, 100 percent certain that you're not dreaming right now? I genuinely hope you agree with me that you're holding an interesting book in your hands, but maybe your subconscious is writing it as you go. Is it impossible? Because if it's not *literally impossible*, Descartes says to throw it out as a foundation for knowledge; instead, let's build our knowledge on something indisputable.

If you're not convinced, let me try one more argument. Consider the following possibility. There may be a supernatural being, or even just an extremely powerful natural being (such as a super smart alien or a super computer), who sets out to deceive us. (When Descartes talks about this being, it's sometimes translated into English as an evil demon, but other times as an evil genius. Some translators and scholars refuse to distinguish between a powerful demon versus an omnipotent god, though Descartes is apprehensive in the text, claiming instead that God is no deceiver and so wouldn't do this thing.) It's possible in this case that this evil genius is tricking you into thinking that you're having these experiences of the physical world, when in fact there is no physical world and no experiences. It's possible that you don't even have a body, and that there are no bodies and no physical world at all. Maybe you're just a disembodied mind adrift in the void of the universe.

You don't have to actually believe that there's an evil demon, or even believe that the evil demon is possible. In the text, Descartes is not suggesting that it's possible; rather, he introduces it as a kind of heuristic, to help you get into the mindset of systematic hyperbolic doubt. You might have heard of the brain in a vat: it's a useful way to put people into the mode of hyperbolic doubt. How, the question goes, do you know for certain that you are not simply a brain, kept alive in a tank in a laboratory, being fed experiences and other sensory inputs through cables connected to the brain? You can see how it's easy to get trapped down the rabbit-hole of skepticism in this case, which is why it's so popular among undergraduate philosophy students. The brain in a vat is not a pure analog to Descartes's story though, as you can tell, since if you're a brain in a vat, then you're a head—or at least a brain—and that's a physical thing.

Descartes has given us reason even to doubt the existence of the physical world. If your knowledge of the physical world comes to you through your senses, and you have reason to doubt your senses, then it follows that you have reason to doubt the existence of the physical world. Even your brain may be an illusion. If you think about it, your experiences—your perceptions, your ideas, your imagination—don't seem to be located in your brain (which is just the lump of cells and tissue behind your eyes, and underneath your hair). Rather, they seem to be located in your mind. It's possible for a mind to exist without a brain and, if that's so, then it's possible for you to be having these experiences, thoughts, and ideas, without any reliance on the existence of the physical world. After all, are you absolutely certain that the physical world even exists?

This extreme skepticism has taken us about as far as it can go. You can see that we've called into doubt everything—you, your body, the world of things and objects. But if we're stuck doubting literally everything, then what do we have? Remember Descartes's goal is to find something—some indubitable, undoubtable truth that you can know with 100 percent certainty—and then build the rest of knowledge on top of it. If there's nothing like that, then the project is a nonstarter. Descartes notices that even when I'm doubting, or when the demon is deceiving, it's *me* that is doubting, or it's *me* that is being deceived. It would be a contradiction to argue that the demon is deceiving me, even though I don't exist. If the demon is deceiving me, then there must be a *me*. It follows necessarily from the fact that I'm having these mental experiences of doubting, or being deceived, or thinking, that I exist. Or, as you've no doubt heard it attributed to Descartes, "I think, therefore I am." The one indisputable fact that cannot be denied or doubted is that I exist, and I'm a thinking thing. Even if the physical world doesn't exist, and my brain and body don't exist, and nothing else can be known, then this is something about which I, the thinking thing, can be 100 percent certain.

It may not seem much, but Descartes gets a lot of mileage out of "I think, therefore I am." From here, he gives an argument that God, in all of his perfection, must also exist, and from God's existence and perfection, he logically derives knowledge of the physical world, maintaining as he does a clear distinction between minds, which think, and bodies, which take up space. Descartes's arguments are beautiful and fascinating and groundbreaking, though in the end, not above dispute. In chapter 6 we'll look carefully at one of the arguments for God's existence, including a similar version described by Anselm and another by Kant. I want to jump to the end, because, strictly speaking, Descartes's argument is not the central point I want to make. What I want you to appreciate here is that skepticism is a real and powerful and healthy and important tool for arriving at the truth, or at least our closest approximation of it.

That is, it may seem like a silly exercise, but it's not. The methodological assumptions, if taken seriously, help us to avoid errors in judgment about what exists and what we can know in the absence of empirical tools. You and I don't have to start from the position of hyperbolic doubt as Descartes did, but we should always examine our assumptions, and then carefully and without error see where the logic leads us. Sometimes it will lead to surprising results, which is the topic of this book. Sometimes it will lead to uncomfortable conclusions. Philosophy is dangerous in that way; once you start, if you take it seriously and you are honest with yourself, you never can be sure who you'll be when you come out the other end. Philosophy is not dogma; if some proposition is disputed by the evidence, then it's rejected, no matter how comfortable believing in it may be. "I believe it because it's comfortable to believe it," has no place in philosophy. Likewise, despite being comforted by them, if ideas are not supported by the evidence, then they're placed in a state of suspended judgment. History is full of individuals who found out the hard way that believing something merely because it's true is a good way to get yourself killed. Western philosophy, which traces its origins to ancient Greece, pretty much got its start that way.

Works Referenced in This Chapter

Descartes, René (1641/1999). *Discourse on Method and Meditations on First Philosophy.*

Further Suggested Reading

Shorto, Robert (2009). *Descartes' Bones: A Skeletal History of the Conflict Between Faith and Reason.*

CHAPTER 3

Hume and the Problem of Induction

BEFORE I TELL YOU about the problem of induction, let's take a very shallow dive into the world of formal logic. Logic is the study of inference and argumentation, or put even more simply, what follows from what. It's the study of argumentation, and more specifically, what makes some arguments good, and some arguments bad. An argument can be understood specifically to refer to a series of propositions given in support of another proposition—or again, more simply, reasons in support of a conclusion. Logic is the study of what makes those inferences from one set of propositions to another good or bad, and systematizes what kinds of rules for inference we can describe. There are many kinds of logics, associated with different inferential problems, or different kinds of propositions. But we don't need to go very far into that. Here I want introduce you to the argument, and to distinguish between two common forms of logical analysis. In particular, I'd like to make you familiar with a distinction between what are known broadly as "deductive" and "inductive" forms of logic.

In deductive logic, the truth of the conclusion follows necessarily, with a kind of mathematical certainty, from the truth of the premises. Which means that in the case of a good deductive argument, if you start from reasons or premises that are true, and you follow the rules of deduction, you'll necessarily arrive at a conclusion that is true. Consider the following well-known argument, which I've put into a standardized form to make it easy to see its different parts:

1. All men are mortal
2. Socrates is a man
C. Therefore, Socrates is mortal

You can see, then, that if premises 1 and 2 are true, then the conclusion C must be true; it can't not be. And put the other way around, if the conclusion C is false, for whatever reason, then either or both of premises 1 and 2 must also be false. It's simply not possible for the premises to be true but the conclusion false. I'm not necessarily saying that the premises *are* true; rather, I'm saying that *if* they're true, then the conclusion must be true, too. The truth of the conclusion follows necessarily from the premises. This is the defining feature of a deductive argument.

The Socrates argument takes the form of what is sometimes called the syllogism, which a form of deductive argument. Symbolized in formal logic, it looks like this:

1. $\forall x(Ax \rightarrow Ox)$ (this says that for Anything (that's the upside down A) if it's a mAn, then it's mOrtal (I use "A" and "O" rather than "M" to avoid confusion because both "man" and "mortal" start with "m." The right-facing arrow just means "if . . . then").
2. As (this says that Socrates is a mAn)
3. So (this says that Socrates is mOrtal).

Deductive arguments such as this one move from universal propositions (viz., something that's true about all of a thing, such as in this case men), to tell us something about a particular case (in this instance, Socrates). So one way to think generally about deduction is that it moves from general or universal claims to infer particular or individual claims.

Some of those universal propositions are what we might call logical truths, such as "all triangles have three sides" or "all bachelors are unmarried men." One does not need to inspect every triangle in the world in order to know that they all have three sides. Likewise, I do not need to meet and observe every bachelor in order to know that each of them is unmarried. I do not need to inspect every triangle or observe every bachelor, because instead I can merely consider the concepts of triangle and bachelor themselves. The great eighteenth-century Scottish philosopher David Hume, who is credited with discovering and describing the problem of induction, called these propositions *relations of ideas*. And you can see why. To discover that all triangles have three sides, you don't even have to inspect a single triangle; instead, you can simply inspect the concept of "triangle" to see that it must be true. You simply observe the relationship between the concept of "triangle" and the idea of "three-sided polygon" to see that they are identical. A person who has never seen a triangle—if such a person can be found—can understand that all triangles have three sides, simply by understanding the concepts of triangle and three and sides. The relevant term here is *a priori*, which is just from the Latin meaning something like "can be known *prior* to experience."

However, *a priori* propositions such as "all triangles have three sides" are not generally particularly interesting facts in the world, and knowledge of relations of ideas are not the ones that are interesting to us in this chapter. Hume distinguished relations of ideas with *matters of fact*. Matters of fact are propositions, unlike "all triangles have three sides," whose truth cannot be known by inspecting the ideas, but rather by empirically inspecting the actual world. One must go into the world in order to discover their truth or falsity. In that way, we say that their truth is "contingent" on the facts in the world, rather than "necessary." The relevant term here is *a posteriori*, again from the Latin, meaning "known *post*, or after, experience."

Let us turn to inductive logic. In an inductive argument, the reasons, or premises, that are given are not meant to guarantee the truth of the conclusion but rather make its truth more likely or probable. Here's the classic example that Karl Popper, the twentieth-century Austrian-British philosopher of science, gives to describe the problem of induction:

1. All previously observed swans are white

C. Therefore, all swans are white.

You can imagine a person reasoning in this way (indeed, you reason in this way literally all the time, as we'll see). A person who lives in a part of the world where there are only white swans, even if he sees many swans every day, may confidently conclude that since he's seen many swans (thousands, let us assume, over many decades), and they've all been white, that therefore all swans are white. And of course, you can immediately see the challenge to this form of reasoning. Namely, it is possible that premise (1) is true, and yet the conclusion (C) is false. All it would take is the existence of one non-white swan to show that the conclusion is false. Those who study such things call the form of the argument captured in the swan example by the title *inductive generalization*.

You may be familiar with the following quote that is sometimes attributed to Einstein, "No amount of experimentation can prove me right; a single experiment can prove me wrong." What Einstein was referring to in this case was in fact the application of the inductive generalization as a tool in the scientific method. For scientists, and those who reason according to the scientific method, there is always more evidence to gather and observe, and always some future possibility of discovering some evidence that finally disproves the theory in question.

The inductive generalization is a very strong argument form, and yet it will always allow you to move from true premises to a false conclusion. And frankly, this is not a defect in inductive reasoning. Look back at the deductive argument above. While the conclusion is inferred necessarily, it's because nothing new is learned from the premises to the conclusion. If you already know the premises, you already have everything that you need in order to know the conclusion, too. All that is new in the conclusion is that the logical structure allows you to rearrange that information that was previously known in a different way.

Induction, on the other hand, is not like this. Inductive reasoning allows you to infer general claims (such as "all . . . is . . .") from particular claims (such as "this . . . is . . ."). As you move through the world, you don't generally perceive generalities, but rather you see, feel, and hear particular instances. You drink coffee and it helps you to be alert. You touch a fire and it burns you. You eat a good meal and feel satisfied. But note that these are just particular, individual instances, that take place at a particular time and place. By touching fire a few times—and maybe talking with your parents, who remind you not to touch fire, you come to believe a more general claim. Namely, not that *this fire burns you now*, but the more general claim that *fire burns*. All previously observed instances of touching fire have resulted in pain. Therefore, all instances of touching fire result in pain.

Notice, then, that while deductive arguments move from general to particular claims, by testing a hypothesis and either rejecting it or not based on the universal, inductive arguments move the other way, they take a series of particular observations, and end with a previously unknown general or universal claim. To oversimplify, deductive arguments move from universal to particular, and inductive arguments move from particular to universal. In deductive arguments, the universal claim is the hypothesis, the unknown, the supposition. In inductive arguments, the universal claim is the conclusion, the new thing that is inferred from repeated particular observations.

The inductive generalization is truly a marvel of human reasoning and logical inference. It allows you to learn things about the world and about causal connections without directly observing them. Because, as David Hume put it simply, "instances, of which we have had no experience, must resemble those, of which we have had experience, and that the course of nature continues always uniformly the same."[1] Consider each piece of information you relied upon to get through this day so far, and how you came to posses that knowledge. Aspirin is good for treating headaches. Sunglasses block out the sun. Turning the key starts the ignition. Tea is too hot to drink when it first comes out of the kettle. In each case, you know these general facts about the world only through repeated observations about particular events of which you have had experiences. You don't need to apply aspirin to every headache or turn every key in every ignition to understand that these general claims are true.

Further, not only are inductive generalizations essential to what you know in your everyday life, they're essential to the scientific method. Let us zoom in and think for a minute how you know premise (1) of the deductive Socrates argument, above; how do you know that all men or mortal? Think about it. You don't discover the truth of that claim by inspecting the concept of "man" or the concept of "mortal"; there's nothing intrinsic in the definition of either of those concepts that necessarily is related to the idea of the other one. Rather, you know that all men are mortal through your understanding of the history of people and your experience with death. You know that all people either have died, or will die, because in your experience, each person has died, or will someday die. That is, you arrive at the general, universal proposition by repeated particular observation, using the method of inductive generalization.

Let us turn back to *matters of fact*. Specifically, matters of fact are established by drawing an inference about effects and their causes from repeated observation that one makes in the world. Matters of fact, and inductive generalizations are, in effect, claims and arguments about the uniformity of nature; there is something that causes men's mortality or causes swans' whiteness. And of course, these causal relationships are not linked through logically necessary connections—they're not relations of ideas. Rather, they rely on a relationship between effects and their causes, which is discovered through experience. And this is where the problem of induction is introduced.

All of the general, universal claims we know about the world are based on a relationship between effects and their causes. And these are all of the interesting things about the world. Not "triangles have three sides," but "all men are mortal," "fire burns you," and "the sun rises in the east." However, let's take a step back, and think about where you get your idea of, or understanding of, the concept of causation itself. There is no "thing in itself" or relation of ideas that gives you the concept of causation. Rather, the human

---

1. Hume, *Treatise of Human Nature*, book I, part III, section VI.

mind forms the concept of causation by the repeated observation that some phenomena tend to follow other phenomena, in a uniform kind of way. The link between cause and effect does not come from reason alone, but rather from what Hume called "constant conjunction," or more simply, the observation that some phenomena are constantly, or uniformly, conjoined with other phenomena. Just as particular causal relationships are known to us by constant conjunction—a ball falls back to the earth no matter how many times you toss it up—so likewise we have our idea of causation itself from the empirical observation that various things are constantly connected with, or conjoined to, other particular things.

And so the way I distinguished between inductive and deductive arguments above (viz., that inductive moves from particular to general, while deductive moves from general to particular) is imprecise. Indeed, Hume would argue that it's simply incorrect. Rather, the correct way to differentiate between the two broad argument forms is to say that in the case of deductive arguments, the truth of the premises makes the conclusion certain, while in inductive arguments the truth of the premises make the conclusion probable. And the conclusions that we infer with probability are based on a relationship of causation founded on some observations about which we know something (viz., our experiences of constant conjunction), and those of which we can have no experience at all.

Let me try to end this section by putting a fine point on it. All of the interesting stuff—the nontrivial things—you know about the world are *relations of ideas*. As I've shown, "all triangles have three sides" is a true fact, but it's not going to impress anyone in the marketplace of ideas. Anyone who understands the words "triangles" and "three" and "sides" already understands that it's true without your help. Alternatively, consider any piece of useful knowledge that you have. Think about how you know that the sun rises in the east, and sets in the west. You know it because every single day of human history, and probably before that, the sun was observed rising in the east and setting in the west. Sunrise in the morning is constantly conjoined with rising in the east, and sunset in the evening is constantly conjoined with setting in the west. You infer the conclusion through an inductive generalization.

But we also know that by relying on the method of induction to arrive at general conclusions—built right into the methodology—we know that while the premises may be true, the conclusion always might be false, since the method of induction allows it to be known only probably. Putting those two ideas together, the problem of induction shows that each of the things that you know about the world, no matter how certain you may be, or how reliably you may be convinced of them, are potentially false. All of human knowledge (or at least what I'm calling here "interesting" knowledge) is either based on a premise, or derived from an argumentative methodology, that results only in probable, but not certain, knowledge.

To add one more layer of complexity to the problem, induction is an inferential method we use to move from observations to a universal inference. If the observations are made in sufficient number, and sometimes of sufficient diversity, we conclude that the inference is justified. And we know as humans that this method is pretty successful; as I've argued, it's how you know all of the useful stuff you know about the world. But if we take one step back, we can see that that's problematic itself, since the justification I give for the success of the method of inductive generalizations itself—i.e., that they're really successful under some circumstances—is an inductive generalization. You know that moving from observation to inference is such a successful method for arriving at new, unique knowledge about the world, because you've seen it successfully utilized so frequently in your life. Your justification for inductive generalization as a legitimate method for arriving at new knowledge is itself an inductive generalization. But of course, that's circular. It looks like there can be no non-circular justification for inductive generalization as a method for supporting inferences from observation. And this is the problem of induction.

David Hume is known to history as "the Great Skeptic," largely on the basis of his identification and description of the problems introduced in the above. Should we give up on the possibility of a legitimate justification for knowing things? Does induction need a justification? Should we succumb to radical skepticism, and give up on certain knowledge?

To see whether an answer can be had, let us try to reframe the questions we've been looking at about observation and inference. The inferences we're trying to draw from observations are universal propositions, of the kind adopted in science, and endorsed as scientific laws. What is the relationship between observation and what we might call scientific law? What is a scientific law? Karl Popper, who we met at the beginning of the chapter, argued that the domain of science and human knowledge (in the broad sense, meaning what we can know about the world through observation, versus more dogmatic domains, such as religion) concerns propositions that can either be confirmed or disputed. Think about it: what scientists do is test theories and hypotheses, using methods that try to show what kind of evidence can be given in support of them, and whether we can think of ways to show that they're false. And you don't have to be a scientist to employ the scientific method to learn new things about the world. If you see something on a menu and a friend assures you that you are going to like it, you can employ the scientific method to find out whether it's true. She can try to confirm the proposition by explaining the ingredients and methods for preparing it. Perhaps it is similar or dissimilar to other foods that you like or dislike. And in the end, you can use your senses more directly; you can simply taste it. What you're doing is testing a proposition—in this case, "I assure you that you're going to like this food"—by finding ways to either confirm or dispute it. You do it all the time.

Popper's idea was to move the realm of scientific knowledge (in the broad sense) away from inductive generalizations, because he regarded the problem of induction as insurmountable, to instead rely on the deductive argumentation method. Think again about the example of mortal men and Socrates. This was a deductive argument. If it really is true that all men are mortal, and it really is true that Socrates is a man, then it follows necessarily that Socrates is mortal. Popper argued that scientific laws and theories are derived more like the Socrates argument, and less like the swan argument.

As a reply to Hume's problem of induction, Popper argued that since all scientific laws are of this strong conditional form (*all* swans are white, the sun *always* rises in the east, etc.), then they can all be tested by trying to dispute them. This method is known as falsification and relies on what Popper and others came to call "falsifiability"; all scientific laws are propositions that are at least in theory falsifiable, because there is at least in theory a test that can be given to show that it is false (falsifiable is distinct from false—the former means that there is some theoretical test that could be generated to show it is false, the latter means that such a test was successful). "All swans are white" is a failure as a scientific law, because black (i.e., non-white) swans have been observed. "The sun always rises in the east" is accepted as a scientific law. While it is falsifiable (we could imagine a case in which the sun rises some day in the west), no such evidence has ever been observed. Or again, your friend was either right or wrong in suggesting that you'd like this new food. Instead of generalizing from particular observations to universal propositions, science proceeds by identifying a conjecture, and then critically analyzing that conjecture, holding it to scrutiny, in an attempt to find a refutation of that theory.

Popper is essentially saying here that the problem of induction, as characterized by Hume, is not really a problem at all. That is, it asks how propositions can be justified, particularly given that they seem to be the result of inductive reasoning, but induction is unable to justify them. It's an impossible problem.

Unfortunately, as a final resolution to the problem of induction, Popper's proposal seems to fall short in a number of ways. First, no one has ever observed a western sunrise, but of course, no one had ever observed a non-white swan, until they did. The skepticism we feel about falsifiable scientific laws remains, even if the rational basis for the foundational hypothesis is no longer a worry. But more importantly, the deductive model doesn't seem to be able to adjudicate between two hypotheses, if they've never been refuted, even if they directly contradict one another.

Above, I said that inductive generalization, in the example of the white swans, along with other forms of inductive inference, was a strong form of argumentation. But I did not offer any justification for this claim. How can I prove that induction is a strong argumentative strategy? As evidence, I might argue that since people frequently reason this way, and have done so successfully for millennia, and that reasoning this way frequently produces useful and verifiably correct results, that there is an indisputable validity to the inductive argumentative strategy. That is, as justification for induction, I might try to show that the future will tend to resemble the past. And thus, the problem of induction lives on.

Works Referenced in This Chapter

Hume, David (1748/1993). *An Inquiry Concerning Human Understanding*.
Hume, David (1739/2011). *A Treatise of Human Nature*.
Popper, Karl (1963). *Conjectures and Refutations: The Growth of Scientific Knowledge*.

Further Suggested Reading

Armstrong, David (2016). *What Is a Law of Nature?*

CHAPTER 4

The Euthyphro Dilemma

ETHICS IS A BRANCH of philosophy concerned with matters of values, understanding the nature of good and bad, and systematizing the concept of right and wrong action. If you've ever been confused or unsure about what is the right or wrong thing to do—and I know you have—then the study of moral philosophy may be able to provide you some valuable insight. We'll focus in more detail on moral questions in chapter 5. Socrates's Euthyphro dilemma specifically focuses on the relationship between morality and religion.

Everyone knows who Socrates was, and most people are at least tangentially familiar with the details surrounding his death. As we discussed in chapter 1, Socrates was known for his teaching method, which bears his name, and which goes as follows. Typically, Socrates would engage an individual in conversation on some subject, usually a person who claimed some specialized knowledge of that topic, and then begin by asking simple, innocuous questions. However, the questions usually led to more questions, until his interlocutor would become frustrated and, usually, simply walk away, ending the dialogue. While his tone was typically one of curiosity and pleasant gratitude at the opportunity to learn a lesson from an expert, in reality the method nearly always ends with Socrates deriving no new knowledge on the subject, and the expert simply not appearing to know about the thing he's expert of. This could be embarrassing for the expert and, of course, dangerous if Socrates finds himself questioning powerful, influential men, as he frequently did in ancient Greece.

The Euthyphro Dilemma

There's a story, told in the Socratic dialogue *The Apology*, in which Socrates goes to the Oracle of Delphi—a kind of high priestess who was known for being good at making prophesies—to find the wisest person in Athens. Why? Because in his constant search for knowledge, he wished to speak to and learn from the wisest people. When the Oracle tells him that *he* is the wisest person, he is suspicious, since as he freely admits in the dialogues described above, he doesn't know the things he asks others about. However, as he goes about his business that day, talking to various experts and specialists as he does, one by one they failed to be able to speak meaningfully about the things that they were expert in. Finally, Socrates realized that the Oracle was correct; while the others knew nothing, but believed that they did, Socrates was uniquely wise in *knowing that he knew nothing*. There is great power in knowing what you do not know.

Socrates was executed in or around 399 BCE, on the trumped-up charges of impiety and atheism, or failing to worship the official Greek Gods, and also on the charge of corrupting the youth by teaching them falsehoods. The Euthyphro dialogue is about divine command theory, which is a moral theory that says that right and wrong are just determined by God's will, which can usually be discovered through divine revelation or sacred texts. Divine command theory is a popular but problematic moral theory that equates the will or judgment of God with the dictates of moral obligation and duty. Simply put, the answer to "what is right" is "whatever God commands."

Figure 1. Bust of Socrates (left). An elder Plato (center) walks alongside a younger Aristotle (right) from Raphael's "The School of Athens"

At the beginning of *The Euthyphro* dialogue, we find Socrates walking to court to defend himself against these charges of impiety and atheism, when he meets Euthyphro, who is the son of a wealthy local farmer and merchant. Socrates discovers that Euthyphro is also heading to the courthouse to give testimony against his father. Euthyphro explains that two of his father's employees got into a fight and one killed the other. The father tied up the man and stuck him in a ditch until the magistrate could arrive. Before that could happen, the man died, and so Euthyphro was due to give testimony against his father for the death of the man who he threw in the ditch.

"Wow," replies Socrates, "you must really have a strong grasp of the nature of right and wrong, and of piety, which is the moral requirements of right and wrong, good and bad. Only a person extremely confident that he's doing the right thing would accuse his father." I'm paraphrasing here. Euthyphro agrees that he is an expert on piety and moral matters. Socrates begs him for his help, since as we know he's on his way at this minute to go defend himself against this very charge of being impious. Euthyphro agrees to help him by explaining piety, which we'll just call right and wrong.

"What is right," Euthyphro explains, "is doing what I'm doing here. Charging someone with a crime when they've committed that crime. How's that for a definition of morally right?" Euthyphro stands a little taller, confident that he's risen to the challenge.

Socrates thanks him for his help, but explains that definitions are like necessary and sufficient conditions. They tell you what is and isn't contained in concept. So if you asked for a definition of "elephant" and I told you that it's like that animal in the Disney movie *Dumbo*, you'd reply that Dumbo was an *instance* or *example* of an elephant, not a definition. If instead I said that they're large mammals with floppy ears and long trunks that are native to Africa and Asia, then you'd be in a position to decide for yourself which things are, and which things are not, elephants. The problem with Euthyphro's first attempt at defining goodness is that it's an instance or example and not a definition of "elephant."

Euthyphro finally does give a definition in this general form, and it goes something like "what god(s) love(s) is good, and what god(s) hate(s) is bad." (For the sake of our discussion about divine command theory, we can put aside the notion that the ancient Greeks had many gods; it doesn't matter if there are many gods or just one god, so long as the definition relies on their agreement about which things they love and which things they hate). Euthyphro considers this, though his definition, strictly speaking, was that "what all the gods love is good, and what all the gods hate is bad." So if there are many gods, then they'll agree about good and bad. And if there's only one, then even better, since there's no one for himself to disagree with.

Socrates is pleased with the general form of the definition, but notices that there's an ambiguity, and in order to resolve that ambiguity he asks Euthyphro, "Is something good because God loves it, or does God love it because it's good?" It may sound like kind of a chicken and egg problem, but it's not. Instead, Socrates is granting, for the sake of the argument, the identification of what is moral with what God loves, but that leaves open additional problems if we're going to apply the definition to particular problems, just like we can apply the definition of elephant to particular animals we may find in the wild. Here, the question is about priority. Did God invent morals? That is, do they exist independently of God, and then when he discovered them, he loved them (due, no doubt, to being an omnibenevolent being). Or, alternatively, did he invent them? That is, did God love things, and through the act of loving, thereby create right and wrong through that action?

Let's step away from the dialogue for a minute, because this is a bigger problem for divine command theory than may be at first evident, particularly if you grant Socrates his premise, which is that either God loves something because it's good, or that something is good because God loves it. To dispute a disjunction, which is a statement of the form "A or B," you must either show that they are both false, or that there's some third, unconsidered option. Otherwise, we're stuck with one or the other of them. So Socrates takes the dilemma at face value and considers each in turn. Assume that things are good because God loves them; that is, God causes things to be good, simply by loving them. But that introduces a strange problem, since God could arbitrarily love anything he wants. He's very powerful and can do anything at all; this is just what we mean by "omnipotent." He could love clubbing baby seals, or telling a lie to your mother. And if he did, then those things would be morally good actions. Not just that, but he could love slavery, genocide, or ethnic cleansing. And if he did, then those things would be morally right.

Now, the devoted theist could just take one for the team; she might reply, "Well, if God wants me to club baby seals or lie to my mother, it sounds strange, but if he commands it, I'd do it, because it would be good." Fair enough, counterintuitive though it seems. The story is actually a bit worse, though, since, in all of his power, God could even love cruelty or greed or murder. But with concepts like cruelty or greed, the concept of badness is built right in. Cruelty is literally best defined as something you ought not do—it's morally wrong. Greedy is something you shouldn't be—it's morally wrong. The badness is built right into the concept. You can see: it's possible to inflict pain or reserve some item for yourself, but out of a good will or for good reasons. But if you inflict pain from a good will, then it's not cruel. Likewise, if you reserve something for yourself but from a good will, then it's not greed. Maybe there are legitimate instances in which it is right to kill someone, but never murder; murder is killing someone that you should not kill. There are no morally good murders. If there were, we'd be committed to a case in which you should do what you shouldn't do. If God loved those things, he'd be loving something that by its very definition is bad. More straightforwardly, God could just love evil if he wants. And God could certainly love something morally wrong if he wants—he is very powerful, as we agreed. But if that's the case, then we must reject the first part of the "or" statement that we've been considering, viz., that things are thereby good because God loves them. In the case that God decided to love cruelty or greed, he wouldn't be causing them to be good. He'd simply be loving something that's morally wrong.

You might try to reply that God could never love evil itself, much less cruelty and greed. But describing the limitations on the power of an omnipotent god is a pretty unsatisfying position. Even you and I could do those things, and we're not nearly as powerful as God.

Let's focus again on where we're trying to get, and that is a definition of piety, or in our case, a definition of good and bad, right and wrong. And definitions pick out the thing we want from among the things we don't want. So we can think of our goal as trying to identify the necessary and sufficient conditions for goodness; the conditions that describe all the morally good things, but exclude all the non-morally good things.

Let's not give up yet, Socrates tells Euthyphro. Just because we've rejected the first part of the disjunction doesn't mean we need to give up on the definition. It's still possible for the other side of the dilemma to be true. And remember that for a statement of the form "A or B," the statement is true if either A or B is true (or maybe if both is true), but they don't have to both be true. We've only eliminated one side; let's have a look at the other.

The other half of the definition, on the other side of the "or" statement, said that what God loves is good, and more specifically, *God loves things because they are good*. Unlike the other side of the dilemma, in which we investigated the possibility that God created morality, this side can be best interpreted as showing that God discovered morality. Namely, that there are independent reasons or causes for moral facts in the universe, and whatever they are, when God comes to discover them, then he loves them, due to his omnibenevolent nature.

Again, let's step away from the Socratic dialogue for a moment, and consider this definition, and potential problems with it, on its merits. An immediate problem is a kind of practical linguistic one. It goes like this: The definition that Euthyphro asks us to consider at first goes, "What is good, is that which God loves." So in simple terms, if God loves things because they are good, and good just means "that which God loves," then by replacing "good" in the definition with "that which God loves," Euthphyro's definition tells us that "what God loves is that which God loves." This is undoubtedly

The Euthyphro Dilemma

true, but we might say that it's trivially true. It's like if I ask you for a definition of the word "blue," and you reply, "all blue things." It's true, but doesn't help us know anything more about blue. Particularly for a definition, it's of no use to us as we try to apply it in the world.

Definitions should be general, and allow us to know whether a thing is, or is not, included in that definition. So if you know that an elephant is a large grey mammal native to Africa and Asia, with floppy ears and a long trunk, and you see something matching that description, then you can infer that what you're seeing is an elephant. Likewise, if you see a small, legless reptile with a slithering tongue, you can infer that this thing is not an elephant. The definition lets you know what is and isn't one of those things. Describing particular instances, and knowing how best to classify them, is part of the job of definitions. "What God loves is that which God loves" does not work to help you determine goodness of actions and choices as you discover them in medicine, business, society, and so on. Euthyphro's definition may very well be true, but it's trivially true. As a *definition*, it is unfortunately entirely useless to us.

That's a tricky case, and relies on some complicated logical maneuvering. But there's another problem with this side of the dilemma that is more straightforward. If God doesn't invent morality, but merely discovers it, this introduces two related theological problems, neither of which would likely be acceptable to a defender of divine command theory. First, problematically, if morality exists independently of God, then there is something that God cannot do—namely, cause things to be good by loving them. This is a limitation on God's powers, which shouldn't be possible for an omnipotent being. Second, and finally, the most important takeaway from this side of the dilemma is that if God discovers morality, then at least conceptually, so can we. That is, if there is something external to God that determines right and wrong, then we're right back where we started, with our investigation of the nature of right and wrong. Learning about these properties of nature is easy for God, who is all powerful and all knowing. He can basically complete this study of moral philosophy instantly. But for us, it is real work, and poses real problems for actual people interested in the answers to moral questions. It leaves open the avenue of philosophical investigation to determine the nature and its characteristics of goodness itself, and also the systematic concept of right and wrong action.

The Euthyphro dilemma, which we explored above, is a kind of criticism of what we've been calling divine command theory; viz., the meta-ethical position that everything that you want to know about ethics—what makes an action or choice right or wrong, what is the nature of goodness, etc.—can be answered by consulting whether or not it is commanded by

God. Ideally speaking, the answers to all moral questions can be found in the sacred texts, or other forms of divine revelation. But if the foundation of your moral theory is simply "what is morally right is whatever God commands," then there are serious, relevant, and important questions left necessarily unanswered by your theory.

Before putting Euthyphro's dilemma away, let us be clear about what it does and does not show. It would be wrong to conclude, based on Euthyphro's arguments above, that there is no God, or that God does not love what is good, or that it is untrue that what God commands is good. These are the wrong conclusions to draw from the above arguments. Rather, it looks like even if God is all good, and even granting that God either creates goodness or loves all things good, still there is work for us to do; if we want to understand the nature of goodness, or to make meaningful judgments about right and wrong choices or actions, we must look beyond our understanding of religion or our knowledge of God's commandments. We may start with a religious foundation, but in terms of our investigation regarding moral philosophy, this is a beginning but it is not the end. What we have left is the careful application of those rigorous philosophical tools to try to get us closer to an answer to these questions. And this is what we'll try to do in chapter 5.

Works Referenced in This Chapter

Plato (1963). *The Trial and Death of Socrates Euthyphro, Apology, Crito, Phaedo.*

CHAPTER 5

Egoism, Relativism, and Moral Philosophy

Ethics is the study of right and wrong, good and bad. But its simplicity pretty much falls apart from there. And you can see why, since the philosophical study of ethics and moral philosophy started with the question that Socrates posed more than two thousand years ago: *"How ought we to live?"* It would clearly be an over-statement to say that there are as many answers to that question as there have been people in the intervening two thousand years. But not by much!

Philosophers generally treat the terms "ethics" and "morality" basically interchangeably. Though I recognize there is something of a colloquial difference between them (for example, you might hear someone say that a person's "morals" caused him to do something "unethical") for our purposes, the two concepts point to the same basic phenomenon, so it makes little sense, and only introduces an opportunity for confusion, to try to make such a distinction. So in this passage, I won't allow for any such distinction, and we'll treat the two terms as basically equivalent. I'll use the terms interchangeably.

Ethics (and perhaps to a similar extent, politics, which is discussed at length in chapter 9) is the area about which, even without any philosophical training at all, people approach already equipped with ideas. Furthermore, these ideas are generally comprehensive, more or less concrete, and often reasonably sophisticated and well thought through. And while many people's ethical worldview sometimes include inconsistencies, or may even be internally contradictory, most people are able to identify the sources of these tensions and reason out an acceptable solution. People generally recognize the importance of having concrete, comprehensive moral principles, and value the same in others. In short, for these reasons I find that the study of moral philosophy is a good starting place as an introduction to the study of philosophy more generally. You live in the world, so you're confronted by issues that you take to be of ethical import, and you act. So you're already a moral agent acting in the world. You already have an intuitive understanding of the difference between good and bad, and right and wrong.

But you also know that moral problems are real problems. The world is a great big diverse place, with situations and customs that differ based on geography, and practices that are based in social convention rooted in beliefs and worldviews that have existed for countless generations. People across the world also adhere to diverse worldviews, based commonly on certain theological commitments to mono- or polytheistic religions, or alternatively based on mystical understandings of effects and their relationship to causes. Is karma real? Does an all-powerful vengeful deity monitor human behavior in order to righteously impose sanctions upon us? Many people do indeed guide their behavior based on perceived answers to these and similar questions.

In response to the complexity and diversity of the world's problems and proposed solutions to those problems, many will lay claim to a belief that what is right and wrong differs across cultures and geographical regions, admitting that because moral problems infrequently admit of a single agreed-upon solution, what is right elsewhere is potentially wrong here and vice versa, and finally that it is impossible for any person to make a full, complete, accountable judgment about rightness and wrongness that applies in all cases. Let us call this view "relativism," defined as the philosophical position that morality is subjectively true just in case it is approved of, either by the individual (subjective relativism), or by the culture more broadly (cultural relativism). Relativism is opposed to moral *realism* or *objectivism*, which are positions committed to the view that there are metaphysically real, or objectively true, moral facts in the universe that we might discover through, for example, divine revelation or the practical application of pure reason. If relativism is true, then neither realism nor objectivism can be. Likewise, if moral facts are objective, or metaphysically real, then we must abandon a belief in moral relativism.

As an example, consider the practice of honor killings. In some parts of the world, a young woman who is accused of some violation of a local, social, cultural norm—such as dressing provocatively, acting disrespectfully toward male or older individuals, or engaging in certain sexual practices—is killed by a family member. The purpose of the honor killing is that in order to erase the ethical transgression, both on behalf of the young woman and the family, she is killed by her brother or father, thus balancing the moral scoreboard.

Broadly speaking there are two kinds of responses upon learning about the practice of honor killings. You may judge that honor killings are always morally wrong, no matter what, and should be banned worldwide, and that violators are always guilty of murder. And this conclusion may be based on any number of things, such as an understanding of the universal value of human dignity and autonomy, or perhaps the harm that is done to all young women in a society that includes this practice. There are a number of ways a person may attempt to ground a judgment about the objective morality of the practice of honor killings. Alternatively, there is a less strong position: you might instead judge that such a practice would definitely be wrong and prohibited in *your* culture wherever you are in the world, but because of a sensitivity to other cultures, or an apprehension about judging those with whom you are unfamiliar, you acknowledge that it may sometimes be the morally acceptable thing to do in *their* culture. Or in any case, even if you personally disagree with honor killings, given your ignorance of the cultures of other parts of the world, you may withhold moral judgment as a means to respect other cultures' practices.

This is a somewhat extreme example, but there are any number of moral conflicts in the world and in history about which you may find it difficult to make a moral judgment. For example, in the West we judge slavery to be morally wrong and abhorrent, but it's also true that until somewhat recently in history, this practice was fairly common and widely received as normal. The ancient Greeks captured and took slaves during times of war, as did others during that period. The Christian Bible documents these trends, and various African tribes would enslave members of other tribes long before Europeans began taking African slaves on ships to the Americas. A person may definitely claim to abhor and condemn the modern, Western practice of slavery, while also being sensitive to the position that while it is wrong for us, it made sense and, therefore, was not morally wrong for those in biblical times, the ancient Greeks, or African peoples before the arrival of those on ships from the West. Anyone sensitive to this kind of argument must admit that moral rules are subject to change over time or place, and thus cannot be objectively or universally true. The rejection of objectively or universally true moral facts is what we're calling relativism.

I think that people come to endorse relativism due to a commitment to two general principles, and so I want to discuss both of these principles, showing why neither stands up to close scrutiny. Furthermore, a good-faith endorsement of each of these principles nonetheless does not lend the support to relativism that they may on their face seem to do. I then want to put those problems aside and show that taking relativism seriously can be a quite dangerous position to hold. And then in the remainder of the chapter, I'll offer an argument that philosophy actually does offer a number of good, thoughtful, and compelling alternatives to relativism, showing instead either that there are moral facts, or at least that there is reason to believe and act like there are.

Both reasons that people may cite as an endorsement for relativism refer to the diversity and complexity of the world, and the problems that can arise from that complexity. The first I'll call the "argument from ignorance," which I can summarize as such: when confronted with some of the most difficult moral problems in the history of mankind, when one really comes to understand both sides of the situation, and really learns that each camp defends their views as earnestly and seriously as the other, one response is to throw up one's hands and say that it is simply not possible to choose which is correct. The formal structure of the argument from ignorance says that since it is very difficult, or even impossible, to know whether X is true, then there is simply no fact of the matter with regard to whether X is true. Vegetarianism and animal rights, capital punishment, terrorism and war, environmental issues—the list of moral controversies and dilemmas is long, and the urge to conclude that there is no single right answer that applies to everyone everywhere for all time is a strong one. But I think it's mistaken, and that relativism in all its forms is a dangerous position to hold, and in any case, belief in it is frequently based on low-quality reasoning.

In particular, taking relativism seriously introduces a number of immediate undesirable positions that most people would feel uncomfortable to hold. First, as the example of honor killings makes clear, it's difficult to see how a relativist can ever criticize other cultures. When one ethnic group engages in a genocide of another, when a foreign government attempts to exterminate an ethnicity, race, or religion, or when a culture imposes draconian practices upon its women and girls, the strongest reply available to a relativist is that such practices would be wrong *for us*. But the ability to make a moral judgment about practices of others would be logically cut off, as the moral foundation of relativism demands that ethical values are culturally dependent. This should sound strange, since as a consequence, one must judge that genocide, ethnic cleansing, or the exploitation of girls and women is morally right under any circumstances. We want to say that practices such as slavery and the subjugation of women are morally wrong, not just morally wrong when and where I happen to live.

Another counterintuitive consequence of taking moral relativism seriously is that there can be no concept of moral progress. In the West, the dominant judgment was once that slavery and the subjugation of women was morally justified, and now we tend to think the opposite. But the moral relativist would have to claim that slavery used to be morally right, if that society once judged it to be so. But it sounds more appropriate to say that people used to think that it was morally right, but those people were simply mistaken. Relativism cuts off our ability to make judgments about moral progress, and seems committed to the view that these things used to be right when they were endorsed by their culture, and only became morally wrong later. Ask yourself whether the practice of enslaving another, or exploiting and subjugating young girls, could ever under any circumstances be the morally appropriate action?

The second reason that people come to endorse relativism is from a position of open-mindedness with regard to the diversity of the world's cultures, history, and customs. Let me tell you a story, recounted in Herodotus's *History* (ca. 430 BCE). Darius, who was the king of ancient Persia, tells the story of visiting the Callatians of ancient India, where the local custom was to eat the flesh of their dead. They did this in order to honor the memory of their ancestors, and perhaps in an attempt to physically absorb their history and virtuous character. When Darius explained this custom to the ancient Greeks, who regularly cremated their dead, they were obviously shocked, as he knew they would be. No amount of money or anything else could convince them to eat the flesh of their dead.

However, when Darius explained to the Callatians that the Greeks have a practice of burning the bodies of their dead relatives, they were equally shocked and appalled: how disrespectful it must have seemed to them to simply toss the bodies of cherished loved ones away to burn and disappear. Again, the Callatians agreed that no amount of money or anything else could convince them to disrespect their ancestors in this way.

Let me tell you one more story recounted (with the above) in a seminal paper on the subject of moral relativism, by the twentieth-century philosopher James Rachels. When Western explorers first encountered the indigenous peoples native to Canada and Alaska (the *Inuit* and *Yupik*, sometimes collectively known as *Eskimo*, but in modern times referred to more commonly as *Inuit*), they discovered a number of unusual customary practices. Chief among them is that infanticide was quite common. In particular when a mother delivers a baby (most usually a girl baby) it is not uncommon for the family to decide to kill the child at birth. Likewise, when the elderly members of their community become too feeble or burdensome, the practice is to move them out into remote, icy cold locations to allow them to freeze to death. This is called "geronticide." These practices are at the discretion of the family entirely, and there is no broader social stigma in these communities against or for these actions.

Now ritualistically killing the infants or elderly members of your community probably strikes you as an obvious moral wrong, just as burning the dead sounded wrong and abhorrent to the Callatians, and eating the dead sounded wrong and abhorrent to the Greeks. But is relativism the correct response? Should we infer that there is no right or wrong answer, and that what is morally correct depends on where you are in the world, or when you are in history?

Let us look more closely at each example. In the case of the Inuit people as they were discovered by Western explorers, the environment where they lived was extremely harsh, with resources that were extremely scarce, including food sources that could only be caught during a narrow window of time each year, and only through extraordinary and dangerous effort. Thus, in this society, if there are too many people who need shelter or food, there will simply not be enough, potentially putting everyone at risk. Just as when, e.g., we prioritize medical treatment for those who are most sick or who most urgently need it, the Inuit practice was based on an understanding that what is morally required is to make choices or take actions that are to the benefit of the greatest number of people. Our modern understanding of moral requirements, which plays out in terms of accepted public policy, prioritizes the distribution of scarce resources to either the greatest number, or to those who need it most urgently. Understood this way, the Inuit practices were based on this same moral commitment to the greatest good for the greatest number. It is not that their moral commitments diverge widely or even at all from our own; what differs dramatically instead are the factual circumstances of their day-to-day lives. And if that's right, then it would be a mistake to point to this story as evidence of moral relativism. Why? Because it's not the moral duties that differ across cultures at all, but instead just their particular factual circumstances.

Likewise, the reader can probably see the error in attempting to apply relativism to the case of the Greeks and the Callatians. In each case, their practices, both of which diverges widely from the other, are both based on a more fundamental belief that members of their society have individual value and dignity, and that this value extends beyond one's death. This moral commitment may seem familiar to you, and you may practice this yourself in any number of ways, from holding on to keepsakes and heirlooms, or building memorials to our family and ancestors. The Greeks and Callatians held firmly to precisely the same moral commitments, even if their particular cultural ways of remembering and respecting their deceased family members are shocking and diverse. In the latter cases, these diverse practices may be based merely on a divergent understanding of the transmigration of the soul (is it in the flesh, does it require an action to free it, and if so, how to go about this, etc.). But fundamentally, we all agree on what is morally required: we must honor and respect those who came before us. What differs is merely how we go about it. That is, they agree with each other, and with our contemporary understanding of moral requirements and duties, and disagree merely about the facts of the world. And if that's right, the case of the Greeks and the Callatians does not support the argument for moral relativism, which says that it is the moral judgments themselves which vary so dramatically.

As Rachels puts it, the moral differences are merely apparent, but not real. In both cases, they typically apply the exact same moral principles, but given different circumstances of their lives, their cultural beliefs, and their surroundings, those principles are expressed much differently.

So if moral relativism—which we've essentially described as the view that claims there's no fact of the matter, or that morality is all a matter of perspective—is to be rejected, what can we possibly replace it with? In the second half of this chapter, I want to introduce readers to some of the dominant theories from moral philosophy in the Western tradition. That is, what follows is by no means exhaustive, and what I leave out includes extremely influential theories from the West, including virtue ethics, the ethics of care, and others, as well as a rich tradition in Eastern philosophy, including Taoism, Confusionism, and others. My goal here is not to be exhaustive, but rather merely to make the case that it is possible to give positive arguments in favor of objectively real, moral judgments.

This story comes from Book II of Plato's *Republic*. While Socrates is the main character here, the speaker is Glaucon, who tells the story of a shepherd who, while minding his flock, experiences an earthquake, which opens a fissure in the ground. When the shepherd climbs into the fissure, he finds a tomb. In the tomb is a skeleton, and on the hand of the skeleton is a ring, which he takes. Later, while sitting around the fire with the other shepherds, he notices that when he turns the collet of the ring this way, he becomes invisible, and when he turns it back, he becomes visible again. With the ring of invisibility, the shepherd conspires to visit the castle where he seduces the queen, and they kill the king and the shepherd becomes the king.

Glaucon tells the story of the ring as a response to Socrates's questioning about what is moral. In Glaucon's telling of the story, not only are we unsurprised that the shepherd would do the thing, but we also, whether we admit to it or not, think that getting away with his scheme is what the shepherd, or anyone else who finds himself in a similar position, *should* do.

That is, if we found out that the shepherd could get away with benefiting himself and he also knew that he would never get caught, we tend to think that he should do it, and deciding not to would be a little bit stupid of him.

You can judge for yourself what you think of the shepherd here, but let's look more closely in particular at Glaucon's argument: Glaucon's position is that you completely understand the shepherd's actions, and that if you absolutely knew that you could get away with it, your actions would always be aimed toward the central goal of benefiting yourself. The main reason you don't act this way in your daily life is because you know that if others see you as a selfish person, then they won't trust your motives, making your interactions with them less profitable for you. For Glaucon, then, what is centrally important in your choices and actions is not so much altruistic behavior that benefits others, but rather a good reputation. What is important is not *being* good, but rather being *seen* as good.

The philosophical position that Glaucon is defending is called "egoism." Broadly speaking, we might mean one of two things by egoism. We may mean to say either that people do act in a way that is generally self-interested, or we may mean to say that people ought to act in a way that is fundamentally self-interested. The first is a *descriptive* claim, which sets out simply to describe how people act. Egoism in the descriptive sense is a psychological principle and is generally known as "psychological egoism." The second is what we would call a *prescriptive* claim, which doesn't merely describe what people do, but instead makes a claim about what people ought to do. This is a normative, or moral, claim, and is generally known as "ethical egoism."

On its face the descriptive psychological egoist position is more obvious. Here the claim is merely that people have one ultimate or fundamental aim, and that is his/her own self-interest. Obviously sometimes people do actions that are not in their best interest (or their perceived interests), but this is allowed by the theory, given that people don't act from perfect information, or perfect rationality. In short, people make mistakes. What psychological egoism doesn't account for is selfless or altruistic behavior, which we may define as behavior aimed toward the benefit of the self-interest of another. For example, while a parent may make sacrifices for his/her children, the biological imperative to protect one's genetic legacy shows a self-interested motivation. Even Mother Teresa, who might be regarded as a model for so-called altruistic behavior, acted as she did because she wanted to please her God, and from an understanding of what he demanded in order for her to gain entrance to an eternal afterlife. Read this way, from the perspective of psychological egoism, even Mother Teresa's motives were selfish in the end.

There are cases that are a bit harder for the psychological egoist to explain, such as when a soldier sacrifices his life by throwing himself on a grenade, to protect the lives of others. If asked, the soldier might respond that the reason for the action was to benefit others, or because he perceived it to be his duty. But it does seem ridiculous to suggest that he did this to benefit himself. The psychological egoist may try to defend his position by arguing that the soldier's action didn't benefit himself and that he didn't even perceive that it might benefit him, but rather he did it because he wanted to, and doing what one wants to do at the time is a matter of satisfying one's preferences. This is no doubt true, but it risks rendering psychological egoism a trivial theory, since it would be reduced to a theory that says simply that people *want* to do what they *prefer* to do.

However, this chapter is focused not on psychological explanations for our actions, but rather on our moral duties. So instead, let us turn to the prescriptive model of ethical egoism, which is not the position that people *do* act in a way that is fundamentally self-interested, but rather, as Glaucon argued above, they *should* act only in a way that they perceive will maximize their self-interest.

One thing that will be immediately obvious is how different ethical egoism is (or seems to be) from more common moral principles with which most people are familiar. For example, more familiar conceptions of morality may include references to self-sacrifice, or the benefit of others, or the recognition of dignity and respect for other people. But none of that is explicitly included in egoism. However, in practical application a strong conception of ethical egoism may not differ a great deal from most people's moral intuitions. Consider for example that a successful life requires the willing cooperation of others, and the best (or in many cases only) way to ensure that is to act in a way so as to give weight to the needs and interests of others. If I'm known to be a person who lies, or steals, or breaks promises, then others may not cooperate with me. If my actions are overtly and publicly selfish, then my own interests are diminished. And so generally, my self interest is maximized by cultivating a good public reputation.

Egoism is a moral theory that is committed to the view that what is morally right can be determined by looking at the outcomes, or consequences of our actions. If you're not satisfied that ethical egoism picks out the right moral facts, you may still be open to the idea that moral rightness or wrongness can depend entirely or at least partially on the outcomes or consequences or our actions.

Consider the following well known thought experiment, known as the trolley problem. You are the driver of a trolley car, and you notice that on the track ahead of you are five workers. You pull the brake, but nothing happens, and you move rapidly toward the five men, who will be killed without the brake. However, as an alternative, you notice that the track diverts, and there on that second track is one worker. If you act to divert the train to the second track, the one man will be killed, but the five will be saved. Assume that none of the men can be alerted (your trolley bell is also disabled, etc.), and that so far as you know, each of the workers is innocent (put aside questions about whether the five are criminals, etc.). Should you perform the action to divert the train? Should you sacrifice the one to save the many?

The trolley problem as a thought experiment works because of a tension between two competing moral intuitions by identifying a place where they can't both be obviously right. On the one hand, we tend to think that the right action, all things equal, is the one that tends to bring the greatest benefit to the greatest number of people. Consider the way we allocate public resources, or distribute environmental impact, etc., and the idea is that the best way to organize these expenditures is the way that the most people are benefited from them (or the least people are harmed). On the other hand, all things equal, we also believe that right actions are the ones that respect individual autonomy of choice, and wrong actions are those that exploit or harm individuals, or at least treat them in a way that they don't or wouldn't consent to be treated. Think about habeas corpus or the rules of due process or other legal maneuvers to ensure that the individual is always protected from our system of justice. No one likes to be exploited, or lost in a larger system to benefit others at their own expense. The above case—the moral dilemma at the heart of the trolley problem—plays on the tension between these two competing moral intuitions, both of which have strong traditions in the history of moral philosophy.

Consequentialism is the moral theory that actions can be best judged as morally right or wrong based on the consequences of those actions. Egoism, which we discussed above, is a consequentialist moral philosophy. But the most dominant consequentialist moral theory is known as "utilitarianism," which argues that actions are right as they tend to maximize overall happiness, and wrong as they do the reverse. According to this theory actions should be judged by the extent to which they increase the aggregate overall happiness or pleasure, measured in the highest quality terms, for the greatest number of people involved. The most well-known defenders of utilitarianism were the nineteenth-century British philosopher John Stuart Mill and, earlier, his teacher Jeremy Bentham. For Bentham, the solution to moral problems was simply to look at the kinds of creatures that people are, and what motivates every action we undertake. Nature has given us a strong desire to seek pleasure and to avoid pain, and, broadly speaking, everything that anyone ever does is governed by the belief that pursuing an action is beneficial because, in one way or another, it will either bring about greater pleasure or else avoid greater pain.

Mill expanded on these and other arguments. Since we all desire our own happiness, then happiness must be desirable generally. And so general happiness is to be desired. In addition, Mill clarified one important element of utilitarianism, and that is the response to the objection that, if all that morality requires is that we maximize overall happiness and pleasure, then utilitarianism is simply a moral theory for swine. Pigs, after all, are quite happy eating trash, having sex, and laying around in mud and filth. And quite frankly, if utilitarianism simply requires the maximization of pleasure, it is difficult to see a better life for people than simply acting like pigs. Call this the "swinish objection," on the basis that utilitarianism treats us as no better than pigs.

Mill responded to the swinish objection by showing that people are capable of two kinds of pleasure. There are the lower pleasures, which are temporary, fleeting physical pleasures, such as those enjoyed by pigs *and* people. But there are higher, less temporary, or more permanent pleasures, and these are the provenance of people alone. These intellectual pleasures include the mastery of some difficult task, the satisfaction of a long-term goal, or the pleasure derived from the cultivation of life-long friendships. Notice an obvious difference: physical pleasures begin to become tedious or even painful if carried out for any duration (think about your favorite physical pleasure, and then think about doing it non-stop for hours or even days). But the intellectual pleasures are not temporary in this way, leading us to believe that they are higher quality pleasures. And as these are higher in quality, they are the relevant pleasures associated with the utilitarian calculus, overcoming the swinish objection.

For those seeking an alternative to moral relativism, but who are still not satisfied with egoism or utilitarianism, there is a category of moral theory that rejects the view that judgments about moral right and wrong can legitimately be found by looking at the consequences of our choices and actions. In the forefront is the moral theory known at "deontology."

Deontology is most closely associated with the eighteenth-century German philosopher Immanuel Kant. Kant was so concerned about the problems and defects of consequentialist moral theories like egoism and utilitarianism that it caused him to write and develop his own alternative theory. Kant argued that instead of ends like happiness or pleasure, instead the only thing that is good without qualification is a good will. Any of the other so-called virtues, such as courage, or temperance, or intelligence etc., may be used for evil. Lex Luthor, the infamous villain and foe of Superman, was very intelligent, and very brave, and he had many other so-called virtues. But in the case of Lex Luthor, he was able to use each of these characteristics for evil. A good will on the other hand is unique in that it cannot be used for evil; one cannot intentionally use a good will in that way. And Kant tells us that it's easy to see when one acts from a good will: one acts from a good will when one's actions are both *from* and *in accordance with* one's duty.

Now you may ask what it means to act either *from* or *in accordance with* your duty, and what is the difference between them. Think about the case of a shopkeeper in a candy store. A small child comes in, chooses some candy, and puts a large denomination bill on the counter. The shopkeeper selects the correct charge, makes correct change, and sends the child away. But a child is easy to cheat; why did the shopkeeper make the correct change when he could have kept a bit extra for himself? For the Kantian deontologist, reasons matter. If the shopkeeper made correct change only because he worried that the child's parents may learn of the indiscretion, leading to legal troubles and harm to his reputation, then while his actions were *in accordance with* his duty (that is, were consistent with his duty), he didn't do it because it's his duty, but rather for some external reasons. Kant may argue that he did the correct thing, but not for the right reason, meaning his actions were not strictly morally praiseworthy. An egoist may do the correct thing in order to build or maintain a good reputation, but he doesn't act for the right reason. On the other hand, if the shopkeeper strives always to make the correct change for all customers all the time, due to a sense of mutual respect for others, or simply because of adherence to correct moral values, then the Kantian deontologist would argue that his actions were not only *in accordance with* his duty, but also done *from* his duty. For this moral position, reasons matter.

At this stage, you may agree that you can see the importance of doing the right thing for the right reason, and yet remain unclear about how to know exactly what is the right thing? That is, it may seem that the Kantian deontologist is leaving it up to you to decide what is morally right (so long as you do the morally right thing for the right reason). But this is not the case at all; when Kant argues that you must act both in accordance with and from your duty, there is a very specific guide to understanding your moral duty. Kant called this the *categorical imperative*, and to see how it works, just think about what you want moral duties to do and what you want them to be like. When something is morally required of you—when it's a duty—it doesn't matter who you are, or what era you live in, or where on earth you're located. If something is morally right, it's right for everyone, all the time, no matter what. Likewise if something is morally wrong, then it's wrong for everyone, all the time, no matter what. These things are "imperative," meaning that they're things you have to do. Some imperatives depend on what you want or (in the language more familiar to consequentialists) what ends you want to achieve. For example, if you want to board the aircraft at noon, you must arrive to the airport two hours early. There's no moral duty to fly on an airplane, but given the hypothetical position that you do want to achieve this end, then the imperative of "arrive two hours early" would apply. Kant calls these "hypothetical imperatives."

Some imperatives, such as the flight example, depend on what you want. And some imperatives apply no matter what. Kant called these latter duties "categorical imperatives," because they apply categorically, rather than hypothetically. Kant defined this categorical imperative—or a duty that applies to everyone, all the time, no matter what, like this: "act only so that you can will that the maxim of your action be universalizable."[1] A definition like that takes a little bit of unpacking, but it's not too difficult to see how it works. "Willing" is simply an action in which you actively want or desire something, and a "maxim" is the principle or rule upon which a person acts. Whenever you act, that action is based on a principle (unless it's random, in which case it's not based on your will). You eat when you're hungry because of a rule or principle, such as "eating food satiates hunger." Any particular act of eating is guided by this more general rule or principle. And this applies to all of your actions. And of course, being "universalizable" captures the intuition that the application of these rules should apply to everyone, all the time, no matter what; if the principle is not something you can't actively wish or will that everyone do all the time, then it violates the categorical imperative, and it's not morally permitted.

Figure 1. Plato (left) John Stuart Mill (center) Immanuel Kant (right)

An example from Kant: you might be tempted to tell a small lie in order to benefit yourself in the short term, such as, "I'll pay my full rent

1. Kant, *Groundwork*, 48.

next month when my first check comes in" (assume here that you know that there's no check, and you will not be able to pay). Let's attempt to apply the categorical imperative to see what happens. First, what's the maxim? It's something like "tell a lie when it benefits you." What would happen if you actively willed that everyone act this way (that is, you "universalized" the maxim)? What would happen is that every time someone knows the truth, then what they utter would be the opposite. But since they know that you know that what they're uttering is the opposite, then they're failing to tell a lie, so they'd have to utter the opposite of that. But that's the truth, which would violate the maxim, so they'd have to utter the opposite. . . . You can see the impossible contradiction unfold, and it is as Kant predicted: You cannot possibly will that the maxim of the action under consideration here be universalizable. It literally results in an impossible contradiction. For that reason, it fails the categorical imperative and is unethical. The categorical imperative entails a full prohibition against telling a lie.

I suggested that the trolley problem is interesting because it rests on the tension between two competing moral theories. On the one hand, utilitarianism would prescribe that the action that brings the greatest happiness to the greatest number is the correct one, so you should always and without any hesitation throw the switch. And on the other hand we know that deontology requires acting only from a good will, meaning that it endorses only actions that can be universalized, and which treat a person as an end rather than a mere means. To this day philosophers argue about which of these principles is correct, or whether there is indeed a separate theory that better captures our moral intuitions. The reason to inspect both of these moral theories is not strictly to decide right now—as the trolley problem shows, there is disagreement and a tension in our moral intuitions. Rather a useful conclusion to draw from this discussion is that it is possible not only to reject moral relativism, but also to replace it with substantially sophisticated theories that get to the heart of what we consider to be our moral duties to one another.

Works Referenced in This Chapter

Rachels, James, and Stuart Rachels (1986). *The Elements of Moral Philosophy*.
Kant, Immanuel (1785/2018). *Groundwork for the Metaphysics of Morals*.
Mill, John S. (1863/2007). *Utilitarianism, Liberty & Representative Government*.
Herodotus (430 BCE/1999). *Histories Book VIII*.

Further Suggested Readings

Midgley, Mary (1981). *Trying Out One's New Sword*.

CHAPTER 6

The Ontological Argument for the Existence of God

WHETHER OR NOT GOD exists, and whether there can be some logical proof to demonstrate this, has captured the attention of philosophers for literally thousands of years. Some, of course, suggest that no logical proof need be given, or even can be given, to demonstrate God's existence. The nineteenth-century Danish philosopher Søren Kierkegaard (notice that "ø" in his first name; a letter we don't have in English) argued against seeking such a proof. Such a proof would be impossible, since God's existence, paradoxically, entails a number of logical problems for those committed to this method. Indeed, Kierkegaard argued, belief in God required a kind of "suspension" of the rules of reason and logic; instead, belief in God requires a leap of faith, which entails putting aside what you can *know* to be true, and embrace additionally what you merely *believe* to be true, possibly without any evidence at all (or at least without any of what we would typically call evidence).

Kierkegaard's position will sit uncomfortably with some, who want a more precise logical grounding or foundation on which to build their faith out of reason. How, for example, can you *argue* with faith? Logic is a tool that's not really up to the task of disputing or confirming faith. Instead, there have historically been a number of strategies for giving a logical proof for the existence of God. A logical proof does not depend on subjective experience or appeal to what one merely happens to believe. Instead, it can convince someone to believe a thing—in this case the existence of God—who may previously have been unconvinced. A number of inductive proofs may be familiar to the reader. Blaise Pascal, the nineteenth-century French philosopher and novelist, for example, argued we should "wager" that God exists, since if you believe and he doesn't exist, then you've lost nothing, but if you believe and he does, then you gain infinitely (in terms of rewards in the next life). Alternatively, if you don't believe and he doesn't exist, again you end up with a status quo, whereas if you don't believe and he does exist, then you lose everything (in terms of punishment in the next life). Given the construction of those odds described in Table 1, Pascal thought it was pretty clear which choice you should take.

Figure 1. William Paley (left), Blaise Pascal (center), and Saint Anselm of Caterbury (right)

	God Does Exist	God Doesn't Exist
I Do Believe	I go to heaven	Nothing happens
I Don't Believe	I go to hell	Nothing happens

Table 1. Pascal's Wager

Another inductive argument for God's existence is attributed to the eighteenth-century English philosopher William Paley, which we'll call the argument from design, and which we'll discuss in greater detail in chapter 7. The world, the argument goes, is complex, so it must have been designed by an intelligent designer. Consider, Paley argues, that you're walking through a garden and you accidentally kick a stone. For all you know, that stone has been sitting there forever and you may give it no more thought. Alternatively, if you were walking through the same garden and you pitched your

The Ontological Argument for the Existence of God

foot against a watch, you could not in good faith make that same inference that for all you know it had been there forever. Instead, upon inspecting the watch, it is sufficiently complex so as to suggest that it was designed. And of course, it is inconceivable that it has just appeared naturally by random accidental chance. No, it must have had a designer. Likewise with the universe: upon inspection, it could not have just appeared naturally and by random accidental chance. And so we may infer that the universe, like the watch in the garden, must have a designer, and that designer was God.

These arguments are fine and interesting, and I encourage the interested reader to research and study the standard replies to each. However, there is another kind of argument that is not inductive, and doesn't rely on evidence of any kind. Instead, it is an *ontological* argument for God's existence. This one is initially attributed to the eleventh-century Italian theologian and philosopher Saint Anselm of Canterbury, though it has been brought back out a number of times in the canon of Western philosophy, most notably again by Descartes who, as we saw previously, relied on it as a rejection of skepticism, and to show that God was the foundation of our knowledge of the world. No small task.

"Ontology" is the study of being, or what exists (*onto-* from the ancient Greek just basically means "is," and you're familiar with "-ology" from words like "biology" just to mean "the study of." So we end up with "the study of what is" or "the study of what exists"). As presented by Anselm, the ontological argument for the existence of God proceeds not *a posteriori* (meaning "based on experience"—think of the distinction we've drawn already regarding inductive arguments), but rather *a priori* (meaning "based on pure reason, or merely by inspecting the ideas"—think here of deductive arguments we've looked at). For Anselm, the ontological argument is an *a priori* argument, which demonstrates conclusively God's existence, without looking at the empirical world (for example whether it happens to have parts that work together) and by merely considering the definitions of terms we all agree with.

So with all of that vocabulary out of the way, let's start with a definition of God that we can all agree with. Anselm suggests, "That than which no greater can be conceived," or more simply, the greatest possible thing you can think of.[1] This should be an uncontroversial definition if we're going to move forward with the argument, and I think it is, since the definition doesn't assume God's existence. Just as we can define a unicorn as a horse-like animal with a single horn from the forehead without assuming the existence of the unicorn, so can we define God without assuming his

---

1. Anselm, *Proslogion*, 8.

existence. This is important to avoid giving a merely circular argument that proves that God exists by assuming that God exists. So if, for example, you ask a Christian what she means by God, she might reasonably agree that God is the most perfect thing, and the thing that nothing is more perfect than. Indeed, that's the description of the thing she believes exists, for one reason or another. Fair enough. Likewise, if you engage an atheist on the subject, he may tell you that God definitely doesn't exist. And pressed to describe the entity that he thinks doesn't exist, or to give a definition of what we're talking about when we talk about the God that doesn't exist, he would probably agree that the thing we're talking about, which doesn't exist, can be described or defined as the thing that nothing is more perfect than, or the thing that nothing is or can be greater than. And so on this score, at this stage of the proof, we are in agreement about the definition of the entity that we're talking about, and what people may disagree about is merely whether they believe that this thing picks out any existing entity in the world. Atheists and theists can have a reasonable discussion about God's existence, because they can agree about the definition of the entity that they're discussing. Let's call this premise 1:

1. God is defined as that than which no greater can be conceived.

When we consider whether God exists, there are two things we might mean. That is, the word "exists" is slightly ambiguous. Ambiguity occurs when a word, term, or phrase has two distinct meanings. Sometimes the meanings are quite different, as in the word "bank." This word may refer to the muddy, soft ground at the edge of a river, or it may refer to the institution that pays you interest to safe-keep your financial deposits. With context we can usually discover which meaning is appropriate. Sometimes, however, the meanings of an ambiguous term are more closely related, such as the term "desirable." Some philosophers have attributed two different meanings to this word. In the first case we may say that anything you happen to desire is desirable. But also notice that some things are desirable, such as happiness, regardless of whether you happen to desire them at any time. And so while this term is ambiguous, unlike with "bank," the two meanings are very closely related, meaning on the one hand "happens to be desired," and on the other, "ought to be desired." While they are related, and very closely so, they are also distinct and can be used distinctly, and ought generally not to be used interchangeably.

As it turns out, "exists" is ambiguous in this way, meaning that the word has two related though distinct meanings. We may mean simply that God exists in the world—just like everything else in the world does, like you and me, and chairs and tables and cows and flowers and so on. Or we may mean something weaker, namely that God exists merely in my understanding, as an idea in our brains. It is indisputable, Anselm would say, that if we were to ask the atheist who we consulted earlier, that he definitely has an idea of God, and so the idea of God exists in his mind, just as the idea of unicorns or mountains of gold may exist as an idea right in your mind. In fact, as you read this, there is an idea of God in your mind, just as there is now an idea of a mountain of gold, and so God undoubtedly exists as an idea in your mind (go ahead and try not to think about God right now—you can't do it). Let us call this premise 2:

2. God exists as an idea in the understanding.

Now, let us compare these two separate competing ways to disambiguate the word "exists." For example we all agree that (2) is true, given that we have an idea of God, or at least, admit that others have had this idea. However, if, as the atheist claims, God *does* exist, but only merely as an idea in our understanding, then, at least possibly, there could conceivably be something greater than that idea of God. Consider it this way: if God does exist merely in our understanding, as an idea in each of us, then there is a separate way to conceive of God, which would be even greater than his merely existing in my understanding, and that is if he existed in reality. It is a function of greatness that existence that occurs in reality is greater than existence that occurs merely in the understanding, as an idea in the minds of people like you and me.

For the most part, the above is assumed by Anselm to be true and understood by you, and so he doesn't give a full justification for it. But reading charitably, we can see what is going on in here, and you'll more than likely agree with this assumption, at least on its face. Consider, for example, a master painter, who conceives in his mind a masterpiece of a painting. It will be the culmination of his life's great work. Now ask which would be greater, the idea of the painting, which exists merely in the mind of the great master, or the finished painting, which corresponds to the idea in his mind but which exists in reality as a finished product? It is always greater, or rather it is a sign of its greatness, for a thing to exist both in reality and also as an idea in the mind. Let us call this premise 3:

3. Assume that God exists merely in the understanding, but not also in reality.

Now, I can conceive of the idea of God, and so can you (you're doing it right now). I can have an idea of a being with all of God's properties.

But I can also conceive of (that is, have the idea of) a being that has all of God's properties, but which also exists in reality. Right? That means that while I can have the idea of something with all of God's properties in my understanding, I can also have the idea of something with all of God's properties plus existence in reality. But if that's right—namely that I can have the idea of a God that exists in reality, then (3) is impossible, since God is the thing that nothing can be greater than, and if God exists merely in the understanding, then there would be something that is greater than God. But what's greater than God? Nothing.

Here's the beautifully constructed original premise in Anselm's own words (if you'd like, try reading it out loud):

> Certainly that than which a greater cannot be conceived cannot be in the understanding alone. For if it is even in the understanding alone, it can be conceived to exist in reality also, which is greater. Thus if that than which a greater cannot be conceived is in the understanding alone, then that than which a greater cannot be conceived is itself that than which a greater can be conceived.[2]

Beautiful. Anselm is saying that (3) is an impossible assumption. If God exists merely as an idea, then, at least conceivably, there could be something greater. But by definition, nothing is greater. So God can't be the thing that exists merely as an idea; this is literally impossible, given the way we use the terms. Since nothing is greater than God, and something that exists in reality is greater than something that exists merely in the understanding, then God must exist in reality.

And that's it. That's the whole argument. Let's reconstruct it here:

1. God is defined as that than which no greater can be conceived.
2. God exists as an idea in the understanding.
3. Assume that God exists merely in the understanding, but not also in reality.
4. Premise (3) is impossible.
5. So, God must exist in reality.

Anselm's argument is simple, nuanced, quite strong, and apparently, extremely persuasive, as it has been excavated, invoked, and reused a number of times in the history of philosophy. There are a number of things worth noticing about the argument. First, it makes no use of or reference

---

2. Anselm, *Proslogion*, 9.

The Ontological Argument for the Existence of God 53

to experience, preferences, or empirical evidence. It does not depend on an ordered universe, or your preferences about an afterlife (or even the existence of an afterlife). Rather, it proceeds directly from concepts that are widely agreed upon, and then derives additional facts based merely on those concepts and logical reasoning.

Often when students first encounter Anselm's argument, they object, "You can't just define something into existence. That is, you can't say that God exists merely because I can have an idea of him." However, notice that this is not at all what the argument is doing. It does not claim that anything I can have an idea of in my mind must also exist in reality. No. Instead, it is claiming that this property is true of exactly one thing—the greatest conceivable thing. It doesn't work with unicorns, since the concept of unicorn doesn't contain greatness (or if I can coin this term here, greatest-ness), and it doesn't work with anything else that isn't the greatest conceivable. But while this objection doesn't touch the subtle logic of Anselm's argument, are these students on to something?

One of the best-known responses to the ontological argument was provided by Gaunilo of Marmoutiers, the eleventh-century monk and contemporary of Anselm who as far as I can tell history remembers entirely for his objection to Anselm's ontological argument. He presents it as a kind of *reductio ad absurdum* (the form of which we've seen in previous chapters). It goes like this: Gaunilo asks us to consider a lost island, which is perfect in every way. Its coves and beaches are perfect, it includes every abundance of riches, the fruits and other foods there are unrivaled anywhere in the world. In short, it is a perfect island that you are imagining as an idea in your mind. Now, Gaunilo suggests, let us run the remainder of Anselm's ontological argument. Since the lost island is an island than which no greater island can be conceived, it cannot exist merely in the understanding, because one of the properties of being the greatest of something is that it must exist also in reality. That is, as we know, if the greatest conceivable island existed only in the understanding, then a greater island must exist in reality. But no island is greater than the greatest island, so this is impossible. And thus we can conclude that the greatest island must also exist in reality. But, of course, as Gaunilo reminds us, no such island exists, and we have no reason at all to suspect that it does. And so if the argument as it is can prove decisively that a perfect island does in fact exist in reality, then we should be skeptical of anything that the argument claims to prove, including the existence of God in reality.

Anselm, in his reply to the perfect island objection, suggested that Gaunilo simply didn't understand the argument, in the same way our students with the unicorn didn't understand it. For what it's worth, Gaunilo is probably right. Including perfection among a thing's properties at the very least introduces the logical fallacy of circularity, as we are assuming that God is perfect in order to prove that he's perfect. Including existence in reality as a characteristic of perfection, and then defining God in terms of his perfection, assumes what it sets out to prove, in exactly the same way we would if we described the island as perfect.

A second, related objection to the ontological argument is attributed to the nineteenth-century Prussian philosopher Immanuel Kant, and it is known as "existence is not a predicate." Let's try to unpack a bit what Kant means by that. A predicate is like a property; it tells you something about the subject that helps you identify it, or discern it from other things. It gives you information about the subject. So if you're meeting someone in a crowd, and I say, "She's tall, and she's wearing a red hat," this information helps you identify her or pick her out from others. That's what predicates do; they give you information about the object. If I told you a drom-drom exists, you wouldn't know anything about a drom-drom. But if I told you that drom-droms are spikey, now you know a little bit about what a drom-drom is like. In a room full of otherwise non-spikey objects, you could pick out the drom-drom pretty easily.

Here's another example: I have two tennis balls and I want you to choose one of them. If I say, "One is green and one is yellow," or "One is worn and the other is new," then you can discern one from another, even if they have all other properties in common (as tennis balls often do). But if I say, "One exists, and the other does not exist," I have not told you any useful information to choose one versus the other. Predicates are the properties that subjects have that describe them in such a way that differentiates them from other things. But *existence* doesn't work in this way—saying that one exists and the other doesn't exist doesn't change anything about them that helps you to discern one from the other.

Here is Kant's specific example, to drive the point home. Kant asks you to consider one hundred gold coins. These coins have a number of predicates: taken together they have a particular weight, they reflect light at a particular wavelength, and they make a distinct ring when rattled together. But these predicates—in fact, all of the coins' predicates—are the same regardless of whether they exist in your understanding, or whether they exist in the world. The concept doesn't change in any way if they exist in the world or only in your understanding. If the concept were to change with existence in reality, then *existence* would be a predicate. But since it does not, existence cannot be a predicate.

Kant here is developing an argument from *reductio ad absurdum* to help show the problem with considering existence to be a predicate. Assume for a moment that existence *is* a predicate, and that the drom-drom does not exist. Then we may say that the drom-drom lacks the property of existence. But that sounds strange: how can a drom-drom have any properties at all if it doesn't exist? If "lacking existence" is one of its properties, then there must be something that is lacking those properties. A drom-drom can only lack a quality if it exists, otherwise how could it lack it? This is a paradox, which arises by treating existence as a legitimate predicate that can be attributed to anything.

Like Anselm, Kant and Gaunilo were believers in the Christian God and did not consider a refutation of the ontological argument as a proof that God does not exist. But at the same time, like those engaged in the philosophical tradition before them, they refuse to endorse an argument that does not actually prove what it sets out to.

Works Referenced in This Chapter

Kant, Immanuel (1781/2007). *Critique of Pure Reason*.
Anselm (1078/2001). *Proslogion: With the Replies of Gaunilo and Anselm*.

CHAPTER 7

The Teleological Argument for the Existence of God

IN THE HISTORY OF Western philosophy, a number of strategies have been advanced to prove the existence of God. Anselm and others used logic to show that since God is defined as the greatest possible entity, God must exist, since if something greater existed, then that would be God. Pascal and others employed rational self-interest, to show that belief in God makes the most sense, since if you believe and you're right, you get eternal riches, and if you don't believe and you're wrong, you get eternal damnation. In this chapter, I want to put aside those two argumentative approaches. Here we'll consider what is known sometimes as the teleological argument for the existence of God. "Teleology" is a word descended from the ancient Greek. "Telos" means *end* or *goal*, and, as noted above, you're likely familiar with "-ology" from biology and psychology, from the Greek "logos" which means *rule* or *reason*. And so teleology is just an explanation, or reason, or study of, ends or goals. The teleological argument for the existence of God works by studying the universe, considering the ends or goals of the universe, and concluding that the purported goal of the universe seems intentional, and intention suggests an intender, and that intender is God. For this reason, we might call the teleological argument the "argument from intention" or, as it is very often known, simply the "argument from design."

The Teleological Argument for the Existence of God

The most famous version of the argument from design that we study is due to William Paley, an eighteenth-century British clergyman, who developed in his writing what has come to be called *the watchmaker analogy*. Consider, he suggests, that you are walking through a field, and your foot comes to rest on a stone. If you look down and consider the stone, you might agree that for all you know, the stone has been there basically forever. That is, thinking about the stone under your foot does not require any further thought about how it got there or who put it there. Instead, you may conclude that it had always been there, and you would move on, and no one would blame you for it.

Instead, consider the same walk through the same field, but instead, your foot comes to rest not on a plain stone, but rather on a watch. I think you'll agree that your thought in the other case—to immediately discount the object and move on—is not appropriate in this case. That would be absurd. Instead, given what you know about watches (viz., that they're complex, they have many moving parts designed toward the end of keeping time, and that they're designed and created by a watchmaker), you'll know that it could not have happened upon that place for no reason with no explanation; it was created at some time for some particular reason, by someone who understood what it was needed for, and understood how to create it in order to satisfy that purpose. Design implies a designer.

There are two kinds of analogies used to develop the argument: what we may call a *macro* version and a *micro* version. The macro version asks you to consider the entirety of the universe. The planets, including ours, hanging in perfect orbit, with galaxies and solar systems all moving along in perfect synchrony and equilibrium. Better, our own planet's position in all of this creates the perfect environment for life as we know it; if the earth had even a slightly different axis or orbit, it would be too hot or too cold to support the abundance and complexity of life that we find here. If you were to observe all of this complexity from the outside, the argument goes, it would be absurd to dismiss it as a product of chance. Instead, like the watch, you'd judge that the many complex parts working together seem created for some particular reason, by someone who understood what it was needed for, and understood how to create it in order to satisfy that purpose. Design implies a designer. That designer was God.

There is also a more focused version of the argument from design, which we can call the micro version. It's difficult, perhaps, to consider the whole universe and all of its moving parts. Instead, Paley invites you, just consider your eye. Your eye is fantastically complex: there are lenses and apertures, reflective surfaces, tiny muscles that contract in the presence of light, and so even smaller and more complex photo-receptors that convert light energy into chemical energy, integrating with your central nervous system in a two-way interaction that makes the whole thing function, largely without your being even aware. All of this, and it seems nearly perfectly tuned to your environment and your needs to interact with it. And in other creatures that live in other environments on the earth (wasps and bees, for example, or bottom-dwelling fishes), their eyes are similarly complex, but formed to give feedback to their own unique needs given the environments in which they live and the demands on their activities. Your eye is like the telescope that is made to assist it (Galileo didn't invent the telescope, but in 1608 he did build a version that is the predecessor of one still in use today, and so Paley would have been very familiar with its construction), in that while both are complicated, since the telescope was obviously created by a designer, so, too, must be your eye. And of course, God is that greatest and first of all cosmic opticians.

The argument from design, as we're calling it, is an argument by analogy. An argument by analogy is an argument that proceeds from the claim that since things are alike in a number of ways, probably they're also alike in some additional way. Empirical studies in the sciences often proceed in the form of arguments by analogy. For example, rats and humans share many physiological similarities in digestion, respiration, and in terms of our nervous system, etc. On this basis, it is sometimes argued that since rats have some response or reaction to a drug or treatment, then probably humans will also have a similar reaction to that same drug or treatment. Argument by analogy is an extremely strong argument form, and such arguments can be very persuasive. Given the form of the argument from design, it's useful to briefly pause and think about the form of argument by analogy, and the specific criteria available for analyzing them.

As with any argument, what we want is to make sure that it's based on true premises and that the logic of the argument form doesn't allow you to move from true premises to a false conclusion; it must be true and have good logic. If I tell you that Abraham Lincoln was the president of the United States, because Abraham Lincoln was a squirrel, and all squirrels are president, then you can see that the argument has a good logical structure, even though it's based on false premises (Lincoln was not a squirrel of course, and there's no rule making squirrels president, but if he was, and if there were, then the truth of the conclusion would follow necessarily).

Back to arguments by analogy. Of course, we want to make sure that the premises are true, which is the easy part. We're looking at two versions of the argument from design, and the structure of these arguments is similar:

The Teleological Argument for the Existence of God

1. A watch is complex, has many moving parts that work together, it works toward some end, and it has a designer.

2. The universe (or an eye) is complex, has many moving parts that work together, and it works toward some end.

C. Probably, therefore, the universe has a designer, and that designer is God.

But we also want to try to evaluate the logical inference from the premise to the conclusion, which is a little more tricky. Let us take a detour into a (somewhat) simpler and (somewhat) well-known example to think about how an argument by analogy might be critically analyzed. In 1919, the Supreme Court of the USA ruled unanimously that the government has an interest in limiting the freedom of individuals' speech in opposing the draft during World War I. In *Schenck v. United States* (1919), Justice Oliver Wendell Holmes Jr., writing for the majority, gave an argument by analogy, which I will loosely paraphrase:

> Like yelling "fire!" in a crowded theater, saying that the military draft violates constitutional guarantees against involuntary servitude is dangerous. We don't allow people to yell "fire!" in a crowded theater. We shouldn't allow people to say that the military draft violates constitutional guarantees against involuntary servitude.[1]

We could put the argument into premise/conclusion form like this (the language comes out a little awkward, but it's useful to standardize it):

1. Yelling "Fire!" in a crowded theater has the properties of *being dangerous* and *shouldn't be allowed*.

2. Saying that the draft violates constitutional guarantees against involuntary servitude is like yelling "Fire!" in a theater in having the property of *being dangerous*.

C. Saying that the draft violates constitutional guarantees against involuntary servitude probably has the property of *shouldn't be allowed*.

The first criteria for analyzing an argument by analogy is to ask whether the premises are true—we never want to base our reasoning on false premises. Look at premise 1. It is certainly correct that yelling "fire!" in a crowded theater—particularly if there is no fire—is dangerous, but is it true that it should not be allowed? You might think that it should be illegal or forbidden to yell "fire!" in a crowded theater, particularly if there is no fire,

---

1. US Reports, *Schenck v. United States*.

but the Supreme Court case that overturned *Schenck* found that to be false; of course you have a legal right to say things that you believe to be false. It's legally protected speech. You may disagree with this, and depending on whether you do, you may think that premise 1 is false.

What about premise 2; is it true? Is it true that it's dangerous to say that the military draft violates constitutional guarantees against involuntary servitude? It may be, if convincing people of this results in their refusal to be drafted while there is a war on. On the other hand, of course, what may in fact be dangerous would be not to say these things, particularly if we're interested in preserving our constitutional rights. You may disagree with this, and depending on whether you do, you may think that premise 2 is false.

Now to the logic. First, we want to make sure that the things being compared are not just similar, but relevantly similar. The argument supplies two, of course—that they are dangerous and that they should not be allowed. Are there others? Both involve speech, which will turn out to be importantly relevant, especially later when this decision is challenged. Each involves a kind of danger that is in some part overcome in more modern eras; higher quality materials and safety equipment mean that a fire in a theater is not the death trap it once was, and advancements in military technology and recruiting have largely undermined the need for conscription. And so on. The more similarities that the two things being compared share, the stronger the analogy.

Next we want to look for relevant disanalogies. Even if we agree that both are dangerous, the kinds of danger are quite different. First, yelling "fire!" in a crowded theater will get people trampled and killed in the next few minutes. But making this claim about the draft is dangerous on a much longer time frame, and endangers democratic institutions, world markets, and political and military leaders. Further, yelling "fire!" is (at least in this example) saying something the speaker believes to be false, and yet (at least in this example) making this claim about the military draft is saying something the speaker believes to be true. And so on. The more dissimilarities between the two things being compared, the weaker the analogy.

Finally, consider the strength of the conclusion. Interestingly, a weaker argument is the result of a stronger conclusion. Holmes's conclusion was that we shouldn't allow people to say that the draft violates constitutional guarantees against involuntary servitude. That's a strong statement, and it was a decision that was later overturned. What if his conclusion were, "Maybe we shouldn't allow . . . " or "As a nation, we should discuss whether we want to allow. . . ." Many of us who object to the original argument could probably get behind those conclusions. By weakening the conclusion, you strengthen the argument. Thus, when giving your own arguments, or else

The Teleological Argument for the Existence of God

evaluating those that are presented to you, be sure that the strength of the conclusion is warranted by the implication from the premises.

Now you have the formal tools to evaluate an argument by analogy. Any time anyone tries to convince you that something has some characteristic because it's similar in some way to something else that has that same characteristic, you can ask whether the analogs are relevantly similar, where there are any relevant disanalogies, whether the strength of the conclusion is warranted, and of course, whether the premises are true—viz., whether the things actually do have the characteristics in question.

Thanks for joining me on that tangent. Now let's apply what we know about arguments from analogy to the specific argument from design as it's presented by Paley. Remember that we standardized it thus:

1. A watch is complex, has many moving parts that work together, it works toward some end, and it has a designer.

2. The universe (or an eye) is complex, has many moving parts that work together, and it works toward some end.

C. Probably, therefore, the universe (or an eye) has a designer, and that designer is God.

As with our previous examples, we begin by asking whether the premises are true, and as Paley was no fool, we expect that they will be. It is true, for example, that your eye has many moving parts and is magnificently complex, and better, evolution has provided a great diversity of optical characteristics for various creatures around the world, including mammals like you and me, versus deep sea bottom-dwelling fish whose eyes adapted greater acuity upwardly, where all the action is. As for premise 2, the same can be said for a watch, as anyone who has ever peered into the inner workings of one will attest. And of course, there is no question that the universe, which literally includes everything, is by almost any account, fantastically and magnificently complex in its workings and its many parts.

Working through the logic of the analogy, I like David Hume's objection, which he developed in his *Dialogues Concerning Natural Religion* (1779) (Hume was the eighteenth-century Scottish philosopher who we looked at more closely in chapter 3). His first objection is about what we may call "worldmaking," which is a process that we don't know much about, but on which the strength of the analogy lies. For example, we have a strong sense of relationships between effects and their causes; fire burns, objects fall, physical objects cannot pass through one another, etc., and we know this because we've seen examples of these causal relationships thousands or hundreds of thousands of times. And we know a watch has a creator not because anyone has necessarily observed the creation of a watch, but because we have observed the creation of thousands of man-made artifacts like that one. But the causal relationship of worldmaking is not like that. Even if we had some understanding of the relationship between a fully created universe and its cause (such as a supernatural designer), we only have the one example to infer from. Hume argues that this weakens the argument, on the basis of their relevant similarities.

Next, Hume focuses on the part of premise 2 that, like premise 1, suggests that the universe's many parts and complexities are aimed at some end. Namely, this is the central element of the analogy that makes the entire argument *teleological*. It would appear that, like a watch, which has the goal or purpose of telling time, the universe also has some intention, plan, goal, or purpose. What this formulation fails to consider is that any number of other possible explanations may be given for the complexity of the universe, other than an aim toward some goal or purpose. And of course the central alternative to a teleological explanation for the complexity of the universe is mere chance. Richard Dawkins, the contemporary British evolutionary biologist, makes this argument in his book *The Blind Watchmaker* (1986).

Dawkins's central argument is based on the logic of *abduction* (distinct from what we identify as *induction* or *deduction* in chapter 3). Abduction is also known as "inference to the best explanation." The logical form of an abductive argument says that if the most likely explanation for phenomenon P is explanation X, then X is most likely true. Abduction is the logic used to solve the early rounds of the online puzzle game Wordle.

The argument under question for Dawkins goes, "What explains the great diversity of species as they're found on the planet Earth"? He responds that prior to 1859 (the year of the publication of Darwin's *On the Origin of Species*), the best explanation available is that there must be some divine creator; no other explanation could have possibly sufficed to explain the great diversity of species on Earth. After the publication of *On the Origin of Species*, a better explanation was available, on the basis that evolution by natural selection required fewer assumptions (it offers a natural explanation without the need to postulate some supernatural entity, it relies on causal mechanisms that we already understand, such as genetics, etc.). In short, evolution, or simply descent with modification, is a much simpler explanation, and thus, one to be inferred. It is simply random chance, on an extremely long timeline, that gives the best explanation for the diversity of species on Earth.

This tangent into the biological puzzle is worthwhile for our broader criticism of Paley because of an interesting argument that Dawkins makes in defense of chance as the mechanism for diversity of species. The argument from Paley, which Dawkins argues that he would have accepted before 1859, is that random chance is simply not a sufficient explanation for the diversity of species, any more than it may be considered a sufficient explanation for the complexity of the universe. If you take the pieces of a giraffe and put them in a box and shake the box, it doesn't matter how many times you shake the box; you'll never open the box and find a fully formed giraffe inside. Random chance is simply never going to give you a giraffe, or any other complex living being. Likewise, if you took a very large box with all the pieces of the universe and shook it up, it doesn't matter how many times you do it, or how long of a time scale, it just seems unlikely that you would arrive at the complexity of the workings of the universe through random chance. A well-quoted trope on the matter reminds us that even a million monkeys, banging on a million typewriters for a million years, would still never recreate the works of Shakespeare.

Dawkins concedes this point and goes one further. Even a short phrase from Shakespeare is unlikely to be hammered out randomly by monkeys. Take the twenty-eight-character phrase, "Methinks it is like a weasel" (uttered by Hamlet to his friend Polonius while looking at animal shapes in the clouds). With some very simple math, the chance of these twenty-eight characters occurring randomly from the twenty-six characters of the English language is around one in 10^{40}, or 10 with 40 zeros after it. If a monkey banged twenty-eight times every second, she would need 10^{32} years to get the phrase by chance. A million monkeys have a chance of doing it around one in 10^{26} (for scale 10^6 is one million, and the entire universe is estimated to be about 10^{10} years old). The point here is that the monkeys are very unlikely to type even this short phrase by chance, and the short phrase represents only a negligible fraction of the works of Shakespeare.

But, Dawkins argues, after 1859 we learned that there is a mechanism other than chance that allows for the explanation of the diversity and complexity of species, and that is descent with modification. Instead of assuming that every species derives each of its characteristics not by chance, but by the preservation of successful characteristics, and the elimination of harmful ones, across generations. Think again of our box of giraffe parts, but change the story so that every time you shake it, any useful part stays where it is across each shake. You can see that shaking the box of giraffe parts this way would form a giraffe pretty quickly. Likewise with the monkeys, assume if every time they struck one of the correct keys, that correct value was transmitted into the next generation, then rather than taking a million million million million million years to complete the phrase, it would be correctly completed in under one hundred tries. Dawkins and a friend wrote a little computer program (it's called "The Weasel Program"; anyone can quickly find it on the internet) that demonstrates the process. Give it a try!

That is a brief summary, and it only touches the surface of Dawkins's many criticisms of creationism generally and the watchmaker argument specifically, and I encourage interested readers to seek out his book and think about his arguments. But to return to our topic, the abductive support given to premise 2 is undermined by the very real possibility that the complexity of the universe, just like the complexity of animal species, is not aimed toward some teleological end, but rather is the direct result of random chance.

To return finally to Hume's objection of Paley's watchmaker analogy, remember our final criteria for evaluation: *look at the strength of the conclusion*. In particular, we learned that by weakening the conclusion, we strengthen the argument, and vice versa. Paley's conclusion was that the universe must have had a creator, and that creator was necessarily none other than the divine Christian God. But of course, the premises presented along with the logical inference don't nearly justify a conclusion of that strength. Even if we overlook the lack of similar examples (because there is only one instance of world-building on which we can compare) and the many relevant disanalogies between the two cases, it may still be that the designer and creator of the universe is a member of the vast pantheon of any of the world's great historical religious traditions—think Vishnu, or Zeus, or an invisible and undetectable Flying Spaghetti Monster. It may also turn out that our universe is the plaything diversion of a powerful alien creature. And of course, it does not at all discount the possibility that we're all living out the details of a vast and complicated computer simulation designed by some kind of reasonably advanced intelligent entity or entities. If Paley had derived any of these much weaker conclusions (or indeed admitted that any of them are equally likely), this much weaker conclusion would have strengthened his argument. As it stands, of course, the strength of his conclusion—i.e., that the universe was designed by the Christian God as described in the Christian sacred texts, is simply not supported by the argument that he gives.

Works Referenced in This Chapter

Paley, William (1829). *Natural Theology: or, Evidences of the Existence and Attributes of the Deity, Collected from the Appearances of Nature*.
Hume, David (1779/1907). *Dialogues Concerning Natural Religion*.
Dawkins, Richard (2017). *The Selfish Gene*.
US Reports (1918), *Schenck v. United States*.

Further Suggested Reading

Ruse, Michael (2017). *On Purpose*.

CHAPTER 8

Berkeley's Idealist Argument Against the Existence of the Material World

IN THIS CHAPTER, I want to show you an argument that proves that the physical world doesn't exist. The argument belongs to George Berkeley, the Irish-born eighteenth-century philosopher, student of the philosophy of John Locke, and the Bishop of Cloyne. The university (and the town in which it sits) are named in honor of Bishop Berkeley, though for reasons that are unclear to me, the name of the philosopher, but not the town and university, is pronounced "Barkley" with a long "a," as in "hardly" or "smartly." While the main thrust of the argument is a defense of *idealism*, or the position that only ideas and not the physical or material world exist, Berkeley thought of this argument as a rejection of atheism (that is, as a kind of argument for God's existence) and a refutation of what we'll call *radical skepticism* (defined below). And so for Berkeley, I'll return to these themes at the end. For now, keep them in mind as the two arguments proceed in parallel.

To begin, there are four noncontroversial claims it is usually safe to presume that you believe to be true, even if you're not aware of them explicitly. Indeed, if any of these four seem controversial to you, you're unlikely to be surprised by Berkeley's arguments or conclusions. They are:

1. There would, or at least could, be physical objects in the world, even if there were no people in the world. So you might say that the physical world does not depend on people for its existence.

2. Your ideas about physical objects, such as trees and tables, are caused in you by those physical objects. That is, if you think about where your idea about a tree or a table comes from, you'll probably admit that, at least in part, it came about from seeing the tree or table or hearing a description of the tree or table itself.

Figure 1. George Berkeley

3. Physical objects have two kinds of properties. The first kind are called primary properties, because they're sort of in the object itself, and are inseparable from the thing. These are the properties that are described by scientists, such as being solid or liquid, taking up space, number, etc. John Locke argued that if you take something, like a grain of wheat, and divide it, there are some characteristics that the divided things would have in common with the original thing. According to Locke, "Each part still has solidity, extension, shape and mobility; divide it again, and it still retains those qualities . . ."[1] A thing's shape, or its property of taking up space (i.e., extension), is a property that is inseparable from the thing.

1. Locke, *Essay*, VII 9.

However, a thing has other properties, too. Locke argued that, while they're in the thing itself, they are really powers to produce a sensation in us by means of the primary qualities. So you can see that a thing's primary qualities, such as size, or shape, or motion *cause* your ideas of color, or sound, or taste, etc. Locke called these *secondary qualities*, and they are sensations in you that are caused by a thing's primary qualities. The sound that a train makes (which is a sensation in you) depends on its shape and the speed that it's moving past you (each of which is a property of the thing itself). The color of a strawberry (which is simply an idea or sensation in you) depends on its texture, and its location (both of which are primary qualities). Secondary qualities aren't in the thing, they're powers that the thing has to cause a particular idea in you. It's not so radical an idea, even if the distinction is probably unfamiliar to most people.

4. In the end, when you come right down to it, you have no absolute, indefeasible proof that the physical world exists. That is, if I absolutely stick to my guns and say that we're all just elaborately detailed characters in some superior being's complicated dream, there is no irrefutably certain way to prove that I'm wrong. Call this *radical skepticism*. And despite the very minute possibility that I'm right, it makes no sense to live your life as a radical skeptic about the physical world. No one actually takes radical skepticism seriously, and no one should.

That's it. If the above basically conforms to your worldview, then you're going to like this argument.

Berkeley had Descartes in mind as he was creating this argument, so let's start by thinking again about Descartes. We left Descartes just as he was getting started, with *cogito, ergo sum*: "I think, therefore I am." That is, when we left Descartes at the end of chapter 2, he was engaged in an exercise of doubting the doubtable, to discover what is undoubtable, and where he landed was that he had a mind. He is a thinking thing. And since thought is a mode, or "property," of minds, you can't have thoughts without minds, and so he must have a mind. It is the proposition that he claimed to have known most clearly and distinctly.

But it seems strange to conclude at first that my mind is the thing I perceive best: try, Descartes suggests, to have a perception of your mind, versus having a perception of something simple, like a candle. I don't know about you, but my immediate perception of my mind is imprecise and fuzzy, whereas my impression of this candle in front of me is clear and distinct.

Why should we then think that our impression of our minds is foremost? It's a puzzle.

But let's think about it more carefully. I can melt the wax from a candle shape to any other shape, such as a cube. In melting the wax, I can change the smell, eliminating the fragrance, leaving only a waxy smell. If I warm it in my hand for a few minutes, it's no longer firm, but more pliable. Likewise, while cool, if I tap on it, it makes a knocking sound, but when melted, tapping it makes a dripping or splashing sound. Presumably even the taste would change by melting the candle down. And so neither the shape, nor the taste, nor the smell, nor the sound, nor the feel of the thing necessarily persists over time. And yet through all of this, still I observe the wax on my desk. And so, Descartes observes, it is not the object itself that has necessarily persisted, since its relation with each of my five senses is changed. Instead, what has persisted is not the wax itself, but rather my idea of the wax. Literally, what I know best is not the thing itself, but rather my idea of the thing. And since ideas are a mode of thought and of minds, it is my mind, and not the physical objects of the world, that I perceive most clearly and distinctly.

Does this mean that the wax itself doesn't exist? For Descartes, no, and in fact he takes this as the starting point for showing that we can indeed rely on the existence of the physical world. But when Berkeley reads this, he asks, if what we perceive most clearly and distinctly is our ideas, what use is it to posit the existence of the material world at all? Berkeley is asking a question about *ontology*—the branch of metaphysics that deals with questions about being, such as what really exists. Berkeley sees Descartes's first conclusion (I know my mind better than I know external objects) and agrees. But when Descartes moves on to try to show that objects themselves exist, Berkeley stops. Do we really need matter and physical objects in our ontology?

To begin to see why, let us think about what an idea is. There are three kinds of ideas that constitute human knowledge. First, there are your ideas that come to you from your senses and perceptions of the world. When you look at a sailboat, you get an immediate idea about the sailboat. Second, there are ideas from your memory or imagination. You don't have to be looking at your ninth-grade history teacher to have an idea of him/her. And of course, you can have an idea of a winged horse gracefully soaring through the countryside, using just your imagination. And finally, there are what Locke called the phenomenon of "operations of the mind," which includes reflection, introspection, and the like, and is itself just a kind of perception of your own ideas and state of mind.

Given this, you can see why ideas exist; an idea about a table exists because there's a table, and tables exist. I see it, and if I'm not seeing it, someone else would see it if they were there. Any idea or evidence I have about the existence of the thing comes entirely from my idea of the thing; for an idea to exist, it must be perceived. Since a mind is an active, perceiving thing, and a mind is the place where ideas exist and are perceived, then the only way for an idea to exist is for that idea to be perceived.

This is an argument about justification, or knowledge, or evidence. All I can understand by "an idea exists" is that the idea is being perceived. Think about it: it's the only kind of evidence that's available. And so even if something exists, if I don't have any perception of it, and no one else has any perception of it, then there's no way I can know anything about it, and no other kind of evidence I can give for its existence. And so for example, all I can understand by "a table exists" is that it is being perceived. It may be that a particular table exists, but my understanding of a table's existence is entirely limited to its being perceived, either by me or by someone else. There's just no way around it; the only way to have any understanding or proof of the existence of a thing is to perceive it.

Does this prove that the table doesn't exist and that only my idea of the table exists? No, of course not. But it does prove something. What it proves is that the entirety of what I can know about the existence of the material world comes to me through my senses, as ideas. I think this should not be so surprising of a conclusion. In fact, one thing the reader will discover about Berkeley's counterintuitive conclusions with regard to idealism is that it relies entirely on sensible premises that are easy to accept.

Now let us return to primary and secondary qualities and see why Berkeley argues that both exist only in the mind. According to the arguments of John Locke, which were well accepted at the time (and probably still are), primary qualities, such as shape and motion, exist in the things themselves, and would continue to exist even without any minds to perceive them. We could say that primary qualities are those that exist in matter without a mind, and secondary qualities are sensations that exist only in the mind. Let us look at a few examples.

Grass is green (at least under typical conditions). But why is grass green? Simple physics tells you that it appears green because grass, and other plants, absorb all frequencies of visible light except those that appear green to us. The light waves in the green spectrum are not absorbed and so bounce off of the grass, and when that frequency of light enters our eyes, a reaction moves from your optic nerve through your central nervous system giving you the impression of green. Greenness doesn't live in the grass. It's just an impression, or an idea, that lives in you. The greenness, which is a secondary quality of grass, is caused by the location (in the path of sunlight) and the shape (specifically the particular texture of the blades of grass, and the cellular structure that reflects back certain frequencies of light).

Another example is heat. Hot and cold exist only in the mind, since something that may appear hot to you may appear cold to me. And on this front, we can make a stronger case that heat is an idea that exists only in the mind by performing a simple experiment. Take three containers of water, a cold one, a hot one, and an average one. Put one hand in the hot and one hand in the cold, and after a few moments, remove both and put them in the average one. You will experience two sensations, in which one hand is in warm water and the other in cold water, and yet they are both in the same water. As the water cannot itself be both cold and hot, these properties exist only in your mind, and not in the thing itself.

At this point, in order to show that not only secondary but also primary qualities exist in the mind alone, Berkeley gives an argument, which I call "the argument from perceptual relativity." Recall that size, shape, motion, extension, etc., are the primary qualities, meant to exist only in the thing. However, Berkeley argues, even with respect to these characteristics, the properties depend on one's perception of the thing. Consider a basketball hoop. What shape is it? Obviously it's round, isn't it?

Figure 2. The oval compared to the shape of the basketball hoop

But consider that the hoop, while round when looking directly down at it, appears as an oval from any other position. (This is why it is trivially easy to drop a ball through the hoop from directly above, but more challenging while standing below it, at any position on the court). From one perspective it appears round, and from any other perspective, it appears oval. Why should we think that there is one uniquely privileged perspective from which to view the hoop "correctly"? Why is round the correct shape, and all others incorrect? Why is the shape round, and this is considered the primary quality that exists in the object itself?

As another example, consider a butterfly who wanders on a Trans-Atlantic flight from Los Angeles to Hong Kong. In mid-flight, the butterfly lights upon the seat in front of you, leaving you to ponder the primary qualities of the butterfly. What is its location? Is it sitting motionless on a seat back? Or is it hurtling at 500 miles per hour though the air? Is it in motion or motionless? Remember too, that as you sit comfortably in your chair, the earth is spinning on its axis, moving you in a circular motion at a rate of about a thousand miles an hour. And of course both you and the butterfly on the plane are on the earth, which is itself revolving around the sun, moving through space at a rate of around 67 thousand miles an hour. And I don't even know how fast our solar system is moving in an entirely different direction as it moves through the galaxy. Is the butterfly sitting still, or is it in motion? If it's in motion, what is its motion and direction? What about you?

If you answer that it depends on how you look at it, then you are in agreement with the argument from perceptual relativity. From one perspective, the hoop has a particular shape, and from another perspective, another shape. From the butterfly's perspective, it is still. However, the answer changes if you're on the ground, and changes again from the perspective of the sun, and again from a different location. A thing's primary qualities, this argument goes, depends on the perspective of the perceiver. And if that is right, then a thing's primary qualities exist merely as ideas in a mind, and not distinctly in the thing itself. The argument from perceptual relativity asks that you altogether reject Locke's distinction between primary and secondary qualities.

Let us take stock; what have we actually proven so far? Have I proven that since a thing's primary qualities seem to depend on a perception, that there is no correct fact of the matter? Is it really true that the basketball hoop has no distinct shape, or that there's no correct perspective from which to judge the motion of the butterfly? No, of course not. A better conclusion is that given my perception, I simply don't have enough information to know what is the privileged, correct color of the grass, motion of the butterfly, shape and extension of the basketball hoop, etc. Knowing these things is difficult, or in some cases even impossible. Consider the concept of extension.

From Descartes, just as thought is a "mode" of minds, we know that extension is a "mode" of matter, meaning that matter is the substratum (or "stuff") that supports extension. And so at this point, while we don't directly perceive the matter—what we perceive is properties of things, which we assume are somehow *caused* by the matter—we understand what matter is. It's meant to be the "substance" or "stuff" that *supports* the properties, which we then perceive. Right?

Supports? Let's stop right here. You and I know what it usually means for one thing to support another. Berkeley says that we can think of the way that a pillar supports a roof as a typical way to understand it. But that's not what's supposed to be going on when the matter, or substance of a thing, "supports" the properties of that thing. Even the language we try to use to think about and explain the relationship between matter and the properties in our perception is awkward, and fails. This intuitive relationship that we think is so obvious fails to stand up to even the simplest scrutiny. And of course, for Berkeley, the correct response when faced with the challenge of identifying the exact relationship between the physical stuff of matter, and our ideas of matter, is to be skeptical about that relationship at all. Berkeley, of course, will go on to conclude that we should reject the existence of the material world altogether. At this stage, we have all the necessary parts of the argument in place to see why.

Let's start with a question that Berkeley may put to us: If *being* is so abstract a term, and *supporting* must be somehow understood other than in the regular sense, and material substance must be understood in terms of the concepts of the being that supports matter, then what can we even mean by material substance? Worse, why bother worrying about the "stuff" that "supports" our sensible qualities, if those sensible qualities are merely ideas, and ideas have no existence outside the mind? This is the question about ontology that we looked at earlier—if I have no evidence of the material world, and it's not doing any work as I try to explain and understand the world, why should I believe in it at all?

You might reply that maybe matter—that is, the material substance whose being supports those properties that we perceive in our minds—exists independently of minds. It's a reasonable response. But how could we know this? Remember that we know everything we know either through perception, or through operations of the mind, such as by logical inference. Perceptions we're familiar with—they're just the impressions that come to you through your five senses. Operations of the mind are based on logical relations. We infer particular facts from other facts, such as when we derive that Socrates is mortal from the previously known propositions that all men are mortal, and that Socrates is a man.

Thought experiments provide another kind of operation of the mind. One of the most famous thought experiments is attributed to Galileo, in

Berkeley's Idealist Argument

which he set out to disprove Aristotle's claim that gravity drags objects to earth at a rate proportional to their mass. Instead, Galileo proved that objects fall at a uniform rate independent of their mass. Consider two objects, such as a ten-pound bowling ball, and a one-ounce marble. If they are dropped simultaneously from the Leaning Tower of Pisa, then if Aristotle is right, then the bowling ball should hit the ground first. But, Galileo hypothesized, if they are attached by a string and released, then the descent of the heavier bowling ball should be slowed by being attached to the lighter marble, once the string grows taut. However, because the two objects are connected together, the mass of the entire system is actually *heavier* than either, and so should actually fall faster. But it cannot fall both faster and slower. That would be a contradiction, and we cannot believe a contradiction. And so we should reject Aristotle's thesis.

Now something would be logically entailed in this way because if we assume that it is false, it would result in some contradiction (such as something moving both faster and slower at the same time). This sort of operation of the mind allows us to discover new things based entirely on an inspection of the logical elements and their relationship to one another, without doing any empirical work at all (such as dropping a bowling ball from the Leaning Tower of Pisa). But Berkeley notes here that there is no contradiction in assuming that material substance doesn't exist in the world. The only possible contradiction might be that this assumption would result in the contradiction that matter both exists and doesn't exist, but this would be a question-begging, circular argument, since it assumes as part of the argument that matter does exist, in order to derive the contradiction.

There is simply no necessary *logical* connection (that is, a connection using the pure power of deductive logic) between material substance and our ideas. And so the conclusion here is that we don't derive our knowledge of the material world from operations of the mind. What about the senses?

Remember that there are two ways of knowing things—logical operations of the mind, and our senses—this leaves only the possibility that we derive our knowledge of material substance from our senses. But as Berkeley has shown, we don't actually have any sense impressions of the material substance; what you perceive most immediately and directly is not the stuff that makes up an object, but rather your ideas of the various properties of the object. But ideas are not in the object, and properties are not in the object. Ideas and properties are entirely modes of thought, and exist as perceptions in your mind.

What we've shown here, remember, is not that bodies don't exist, but rather if they do exist, we have no way of knowing about it, since the only way we can know things is either through our senses, or through logical operations of the mind. And still, Berkeley knows that readers may want to push back against his arguments here: it would just be a simpler explanation (and as we know, all things equal, the simplest explanation for some phenomenon is typically the better, correct one) that our ideas of bodies and material substance comes to us through the material substance itself. But even this "argument from simplicity" seems to fail: How exactly are the bodies, or the material substance itself, supposed to get *into* the mind? How can a body affect a mind at all?

This will remind you of the trouble Descartes has proving that, on the one hand, bodies and minds are entirely different kinds of substances in the world, and on the other, somehow they interact causally with one another. Descartes somewhat famously and unsatisfyingly declared that the point of interaction between minds and bodies was the small region of the brain where the pineal gland is located. Your pineal gland is part of your endocrine system; it modulates sleep patterns and other metabolic functions. But of course your pineal gland is a physical object. Descartes's explanation fails to account for how a physical structure (and thus, a body) in your brain moderates an interaction between minds and bodies. And even if it does, this merely moves the problem back one step. What explains the interaction between minds, or nonmaterial substances, and the physical pineal gland in your brain?

Of course, Berkeley's argument benefits from this exact trouble. In response to the "argument from simplicity," he asks you to explain how knowledge of material bodies gets into your mind, even assuming that the material bodies exist at all. Descartes's best explanation for how bodies can have any affect on the mind is extremely unsatisfying and, absent anything better, the best conclusion is simply to admit that they cannot.

So where does that leave us? If bodies exist, we can never know it, since the existence of the material world is not discovered by operations of the mind, and they are not directly perceived by the senses. And if they don't exist, we have the exact same reason to believe in the reality and vividness of our experience of the world. You can see why: imagine an intelligent creature (you can imagine yourself here if you'd like) living in a world without any physical or material bodies, but whose mental experience and existence is just as vivid as anyone's. His or her claim to the reality of those experiences is equally justified, but that claim doesn't at all rely on, or assume, the existence of any unnecessary entities.

Berkeley admits that the test to show him wrong is a simple one: Can you conceive of any sound, or color, or motion, or figure, or any other property, to exist outside the mind? If you can conceive of an idea that exists outside of a mind, this simple test will show that Berkeley's idealist arguments are incorrect. Or at least it shows that it's possible that bodies exist, and he's incorrect and that material bodies exist. He doesn't think you can do it but offers one additional, final proof.

Assume (for the sake of argument) that material bodies do exist in the world. It's easy to imagine a tree existing in a park with no one around to perceive it. But in so doing all you've actually conceived is an *idea* of a tree in a park with no person present . . . all perceived by you. You haven't shown that they exist without you. To do that, you'd have to imagine them existing, but without you imagining it. But obviously, you can't imagine something without imagining it. That's impossible. And by deriving a contradiction, we're forced to reject the initial assumption (in this case for the sake of argument, material bodies exist).

In the end, Berkeley has shown that (1) even if matter, or physical bodies, exist in the world, there's no way for us to know it, and (2) our experiences and perceptions are just as real and vivid even if those ideas alone are the sole content of the real world. If we have no evidence for something, and no reason to believe it, it is not rational to continue to support claims for its existence. Since we immediately experience elements of thought in our minds, and have no experience of, and cannot have any experience of bodies, we should believe in minds and reject the existence of bodies altogether. Belief in them without any evidence or experience of them is simply irrational.

Now that's a lot to take in; the conclusion of this argument is that the material world doesn't exist. But remember from the top, while disputing the existence of matter is the central concern of Berkeley's book, the real and main motivation for doing so was to address the problems of skepticism and atheism. The real reason to get clear on the relationship between our ideas and their apparent causes in things, according to Berkeley, is to show the problem and error of skepticism and atheism. The subtitle of Berkeley's *Treatise Concerning the Principles of Human Knowledge* is *Wherein the Chief Causes of Error and Difficulty in the Sciences, with the Grounds of Skepticism, Atheism, and Irreligion, Are Inquir'd Into*. Let's finish by looking at why Berkeley thinks these arguments disprove atheism and address the causes of skepticism. In short, if the material world exists and we apprehend it via our senses, then as Descartes showed, our senses frequently mislead us as to the nature of these physical things. And atheism is *Inquir'd Into* because while a material world could function without the existence of God, an ideal one (that is, one that contains ideas rather than matter) could not.

Let's talk about skepticism. Descartes fell into this trap because, as he readily acknowledges, material bodies are entirely unlike our mental representations of them. As we've discussed in this chapter, even if material bodies exist, what we immediately perceive is not the material bodies themselves, but our ideas of them. That is, we don't perceive the objects themselves with our senses. Furthermore, there seems to be no logical inference we can make between any potentially existing body and our perception of them. And so if bodies exist, there is both a perceptual and logical disconnect between the material and mental world. Assuming that bodies exist, and Descartes certainly did, was the immediate cause of so much tension and skepticism about the nature and function of material bodies in a material world. If, on the other hand, we reach the simple conclusion that there are no material bodies (because we can't know anything about them, and we shouldn't postulate the existence of something we can know nothing about), then the cause of skepticism disappears entirely. We simply can't be led astray about the relationship between our ideas of the external world and the external world, if the world is entirely composed of mental phenomena. The skeptical project simply falls away.

Let's talk about atheism. Berkeley, a devoted Christian and bishop of the Anglican church, considered this matter to be the primary focus of his work, or at least the central motivation for pursuing his idealist project. Consider this: How do you know that when you close the door, the contents of your refrigerator continue to exist when you're not perceiving them? Remember that what it means to exist is to be the object of a perception, but if no one is perceiving something, such as the far side of the moon, the depths of the oceans, the inside of volcanoes, or the contents of your refrigerator, in what sense do they even exist? Or is it reasonable to assume that your ice cube trays pop in and out of existence as you open and close the door? In addition, and perhaps even more centrally, what is the cause of my ideas, if ideas are not caused by their material counterparts? As humans are imperfect and constantly changing, then the existence of things unknown to us cannot depend for their existence on us. Rather, they must depend for their existence on a perfect and unchanging being, and that is God. The continued existence of the world makes perfect sense only in terms of the existence of a perfect, unchanging, and omnipotent being, who holds each of these ideas in his mind permanently.

Only atheists and skeptics have any need for the material world. What many readers find so notable about Berkeley's argument is that it proceeds so carefully from reasonable assumptions, through agreeable assumptions, using sound logic, to such an odd and strange conclusion. Let me end by quoting the eighteenth-century biographer James Boswell, recounting a discussion with Dr. Samuel Johnson, both contemporaries of Berkeley:

> I observed, that though we are satisfied his doctrine is not true, it is impossible to refute it. I never shall forget the alacrity with

which Johnson answered, striking his foot with mighty force against a large stone, till he rebounded from it, "I refute it thus."[2]

Clearly Johnson's refutation fails to engage at all with Berkeley's central arguments, claiming simply that the conclusion is absurd. And yet I will leave it to the reader to consider what, if any, stronger argument exists against Berkeley's "irrefutable" doctrine.

Works Referenced in This Chapter

Berkeley, George W. (1988). *A Treatise Concerning the Principles of Human Knowledge.*
Locke, John (1847). *An Essay Concerning Human Understanding.*
Descartes, René (1641). *Discourse on Method and Meditations on First Philosophy.*
Boswell, James (1873). *The Life of Samuel Johnson.*

---

2. Boswell, *Life of Samuel Jackson*, 134.

CHAPTER 9

Social Contract Theory

HAVE YOU EVER WONDERED why you have to obey the laws of the state or country in which you live? Not just the obvious reason—everyone understands that they'll face the risk or threat of sanctions, such as fines or imprisonment if you don't. But more fundamentally: why are the laws that govern or constrain your behavior correct and just, and why should you obey them, or why should you *want* to obey them? On the face of it, they're just made up by some people, and those people may have made up different laws just as easily, meaning that the laws currently on the books are in a sense arbitrary and might very well have looked entirely different than they actually do. Why should you be obliged to obey laws that were made up before you were born, by people who are no longer alive, for reasons that may or may not have any explanation at all?

Allow me to oversimplify a version of an argument by an anarchist, or a civil libertarian, who might try to convince you that the government doesn't have any legitimate rights to influence or compel your behavior, except where you agree to be influenced or compelled. It goes like this: You are a free person, born with equal rights and liberties along with everyone else. You might say that your freedoms and liberties are best served by consulting your individual self-interests. And so the government control over you should be very minimal, since any time someone can control or compel you, that represents a limitation on your freedom, and in particular your freedom to pursue your own self-interests. High, graduated income tax or sales taxes, or regulations over private industries are illegitimate violations of personal rights. Charging you taxes under threat of imprisonment is simply stealing from the powerless by the powerful—a form of slavery even. Taking from those who earned their money, in the form of a tax, and giving it to those who didn't earn it, in the form of a government entitlement or social good, is fundamentally unjust and a violation of your personal liberties. Most notably, your individual liberties include your right to benefit from and control your own property. This explanation is clearly an oversimplification—or a caricature even—but in broad, general strokes, this is an outline of how the argument goes.

Figure 1. Thomas Hobbes (left), John Locke (center), John Rawls (right)

Something like the above is fashionable in some circles, and though I think it's ultimately wrong, I do think it's built on something right and important. Namely, the rules that govern the make-up or structure of our society should benefit people. They should work to your advantage. They should derive from your consent, and they should be derived from a decision that is based on your own self-interest, rather than altruism, or an argument about maximizing the benefits of the greatest number of people. The incredibly important twentieth-century moral and political philosopher John Rawls, who wrote on this subject, described a just society as a system of cooperation, or a cooperative venture, for mutual advantage. That is, government should work to your advantage, and everyone's advantage, in some way. Otherwise, why have it? This position has roots in the seventeenth- and eighteenth-century political philosophers, such as Thomas Hobbes, John Locke, and Jean-Jacques Rousseau, who are associated with what became known as *social contract theory*. As the argument goes, a government wields legitimate authority over an individual only if that individual has consented to give up some of his liberties or freedoms, usually in exchange for the government's protection over his remaining rights. This consent may be given explicitly, which raises the concerns at the start of this chapter, or else it may be tacitly given, which begins to explain the puzzle with which we started.

Let's back up a bit and think about where societies come from, starting from a kind of historical narrative. Let us imagine that long, long ago, there are people living their lives, just doing their thing. These people live in a state that is, let us say outside of or before governments, societies, or moral norms or duties. So far, so good. Now, in this narrative let us imagine that I'm a chicken farmer, and that you live nearby on a farm that grows cabbages. In this natural, pre-political state, you and I may come to an agreement—chicken is better in a soup with cabbage, and cabbage is better in a soup with chicken, and so you and I come together to form a compact, or a contract, to make a trade. The trade benefits you and so you agree to it, and the trade benefits me, so I agree to it. It is a system of cooperation based on self-interest and mutual advantage.

You and I are not the only people, and the larger world can be a scary place, of course. You and I know that people in another town would like to have our chickens and cabbages, and that for them it would be a lot easier just to kill us and take our stuff, than it would be to trade with us. So in addition to cooperating on soup, we might also cooperate in a common defense; we agree to form a little society to protect one another from neighboring terrorists. Maybe we enter into an agreement to take turns standing watch against our common enemies. This compact benefits you, so you agree to it, and the compact benefits me, so I agree to it. It is a system of cooperation based on self-interest and mutual advantage.

Some professions, of course, are broader in scope or create goods with longer consumption times. If one of our neighbors builds barns, and another raises cows, they may be apprehensive about trading a barn or a cow for the appropriate amount of cabbage, since cabbages are likely to go bad before he can use them. So we each might agree to some common currency and a market to trade our goods. We may agree that a certain exchange rate is appropriate between barns and cabbages and enter into a market to exchange those things. Entering into this currency-based market benefits you, so you agree to it, and it benefits the barn maker, so he agrees to it. This is also true for the cow farmer and the chicken farmer. It is still a system of cooperation based on self-interest and mutual advantage.

I think you can see where we're heading, and we can fast-forward through this narrative and imagine a rough outline of a society. As it becomes larger and more complex, we'd empower a trustworthy individual or group of individuals to make and enforce the rules that govern our conduct—you and I no longer need to stand watch at night to avoid raids by neighboring terrorists, if we can raise a police force and a judiciary system. Likewise, I no longer have to worry about your cheating on, or breaking, our contract. And our society can have people who work and study in specialized trades, which means that our marketplace includes more and better goods and services. As the historical narrative progresses, we can see the formation of a minimal state, including a government leadership based on the consent of the people. The so-called "state of nature," or the world before this social system developed, would have been as the philosopher Thomas Hobbes famously put it, "nasty, brutish, and short."[1] But we moved on from the state of nature when I agreed to give up small liberties along the way (such as my right to kill you and steal your cabbages) in order to gain some greater benefit for myself (such as a guarantee that you will not kill me and steal my chickens). The social structure we devised was never based on an altruistic desire to benefit others, nor was it based on a system designed to maximize the benefit from the greatest number of people. Instead, at every step of the way, the changes that we implemented were based on a desire by each individual to benefit him/herself, or to ensure his/her own individual advantage and self interest.

You can see that we've also avoided a system that benefits some one group, be it either a majority or a minority, at the expense of another group. The decision procedure guarantees that the society and its underlying structure has the consent of the governed, because they've agreed in every stage of its development. This society will be stable, since change or progress does require the continued consent of its members. I wouldn't, for example, have entered into a contract at the beginning where I do all the guarding, or give away all of my chickens to you, unless I get something in return. At each stage, I only agree because it is in my individual interest, and the same is true of everyone in that society. There is no stage at which any particular group agrees to be unfairly exploited or oppressed.

This narrative does very little to answer our initial puzzle—viz., how do I, today, find myself bound by a coercive government or social system that limits my individual liberties for the benefit of others? I'm not a chicken farmer and (at least statistically speaking) you're not a cabbage farmer, and you, sitting there with a book in your hand, never agreed to any of these things. Even if it did historically happen the way I describe it—and that's a big "if," since it almost certainly never happened that way—what does this narrative tell us about our own contemporary situation? In this narrative, we all explicitly agreed at each stage that we gave away some right or liberty. Does the social contract require an explicit agreement in order to be legitimate?

The twentieth-century political philosopher John Rawls proposed a thought experiment (we discussed thought experiments—what they're for and how they work—in chapter 1), in order to try to answer this question. He

---

1. Hobbes, *Leviathan*, part 1, chapter 13, para. 9.

wanted to propose a procedure to determine what a just system would look like, and under such a system what the principles of justice would require of each person. His idea was that it is not strictly necessary for you to explicitly agree to rules of cooperation during your lifetime, if we can figure out what those rules of cooperation would be. That is, if we can determine what you *would* agree to *if* you had the chance, then it doesn't matter that you never did agree to them since, given the chance, you would do so. And since you would agree when given the chance, we can consider those principles as just and as having your tacit, or implicit agreement. The thought experiment is designed to pick out the principles that you would explicitly agree to and, once they're identified, we'd know that they therefore deserve your implicit cooperation.

In our narrative, remember, we arrive at a stable system, because at every point we had the cooperation of each individual involved. And each individual in the society decided to cooperate because of the benefit to himself in doing so. Why, after all, would I agree to such a system merely to benefit other people, regardless of whether or not it would harm me? I *may* decide to be altruistic in my decision making, but there's no reason to assume that I will, and there's no requirement that I act selflessly or altruistically, and so we should reject that as a premise in the argument. At no point should we assume or require that an individual would or should give up something for nothing. What we want, then, is a procedure to jump to the end, to determine what are the principles that would guide the sort of society people would agree to participate in, if they had the choice to do so. The chicken and cabbage society was just, and everyone was happy with it, or at least everyone understood that they're better with it than without it. Can we abstract away chickens and cabbages, and just distill down the general procedure for discovering the principles governing any just society? If the procedure is successful, then the principles that are derived would be just; they're such that any social system that does conform to them would be legitimate, and any social system that doesn't conform to them would not command the legitimate participation of each individual.

So where do we start? Since we want to arrive at principles that everyone would agree to, regardless of their particular social, psychological, or economic circumstances, Rawls proposes that you imagine a group of people coming together in the initial state of nature, but those people don't know their particular social, psychological, or economic circumstances; or rather as we imagine them, we don't know the particular circumstances of each individual. In this way, the thought experiment reminds us not to leave anyone out of the deliberation. We're not acting on behalf of the chicken farmers to the exclusion of the cabbage farmers. And, of course, we're not acting on behalf of men to the exclusion of women, or on behalf of Catholics to the exclusion of Jews, etc. By abstracting away the particulars of their situation, we're sure that the story we tell in the thought experiment includes everyone involved.

The individuals in our thought experiment also don't know the makeup of the society in which they will live. Will you have lots of cabbages or only a few? Will there be an abundance of farmers or only one? More specifically, in the actual society where people live, some may be rich and some may be poor, some may be white, and others non-white. Some may be Catholic, others Jewish, and still others not committed to any religious framework. The society that people actually inhabit has some definite answer to these questions, but to avoid favoring or disfavoring any group we do not make any assumptions. This is left as an unknown during the deliberation, since you would not want to include as an assumption or principle some element that any individual might reject. As the members of this original position deliberate, the principles that they agree to would be fair. The design of the procedure that creates the system guarantees it.

Rawls calls this part of the thought experiment the "veil of ignorance"; hypothetical individuals, suitably epistemically constrained, would derive principles that cannot be designed to benefit members of their own group at the expense of members of other groups. They would not agree, for example, to a rule in society which says that women should earn only 77 percent of what a man does for the same work, since once they emerge from the veil of ignorance, there's some chance that they would be a woman. Why would you agree to a principle that has some chance of harming you? Similar questions apply more generally, and so there would be no common agreement to any system that is biased against any group of individuals, nor one that gives unfair preference to one group over another.

If the thought experiment is doing its job so far, the parties in the original position, behind the veil of ignorance, should be able to pick out those principles that each member of a society would agree to if they could, because as we've created it, each principle has the greatest chance of benefiting him or her, or else each principle would have the least chance of harming him or her. So how would they decide? We already agreed, above, that there's no reason to assume that they'll decide to give away their own rights and liberties or property to benefit others or the majority. So we have rejected that as a premise. We've already agreed that they want to benefit themselves. But how can an individual ensure that the principles chosen will benefit him/herself if during the decision procedure he/she doesn't know any of the salient facts about him/herself, or about the makeup of the society as a whole? What would you choose? You couldn't just say "people like me should get a million bucks!," since, according to the setup of the thought experiment, you don't know what kind of person you'll be. And no cheating by saying, "tall people should get a million bucks," since, while you might hope you'll be tall, you may not be.

You'll want to ensure that people in your society are rewarded for hard work, or are able at least to be the beneficiary of their own labor. That is, economic inequalities are certainly just, when they are the result of something that you do, because we want talented or hard-working people to benefit from their actions. But we'd think that they're not just if they're based on something that you didn't do; we'd want to avoid wealth or privilege being attached to characteristics that are outside of our control, such as being tall, or being a member of some ethnic class or gender. And so here is a principle that Rawls thinks that the individuals will come to endorse in the veil of ignorance:

> Social and economic inequalities are just if they are attached to office and positions available to everyone.[2]

This is simply a principle of fair equality of opportunity. Anyone can be president. Anyone can work hard and make a million bucks. And my hard work is equal in value to your hard work, regardless of who we are in the real society. What would violate this principle would be a social or economic inequality that is attached to an office or position that is open to some, but closed to others. We may want our society to reward doctors and lawyers, and yet leave other occupations or practices on the low end of the wage scale. But if we close off those occupations to women, then we violate this principle of fair equality of opportunity, and thus violate the principles of justice.

Societies often contain rich people and poor people. Before you get there, you don't know which one you'll be, but you know it's much better to be a rich person than it is to be a poor person. Conversely, you know that being a poor person is much worse; your desire to avoid being poor is greater than your desire to be rich. A poor person should have no objection to there being rich people—particularly since you wouldn't mind being one and, in any case, you're already committed to the principle whereby people's outcomes are tied to their efforts and talents. Furthermore, a system that prohibits economic inequalities altogether may stifle growth, creativity, and innovation since, as we know, many people try new and innovative things at the promise of the rewards at the end. But behind the veil, an individual couldn't know whether he's going to be a creative innovator or a low-wage worker. So when I envision my consent of the inequality associated with innovation, while I endorse it and want it to exist, I want to avoid a scenario

---

2. Rawls, *Theory of Justice*, 53.

whereby those with the abilities to do so reap all the rewards, while everyone else earns none. Not everyone has the aptitude or skill to be a doctor, or a lawyer, or an innovator. And so here is another principle that Rawls thinks we'll come to endorse in the veil of ignorance:

> Social and economic inequalities are just if they are to the benefit of everyone, and in particular the least advantaged members of society.[3]

This is simply a principle that defines the kinds of difference that we approve of. Rawls calls it the *difference principle*. By benefiting everyone, no individual has any incentive to object to an unequal distribution, since its elimination would harm himself. Imagine a graduated form of income tax, in which those who earn more pay a higher percentage into the system. Under such a system, why would I object that you earn more than I do? If I insist that you should be paid the same as me for different work, I would be harming myself, because in that case common goods and resources, paid for by an income tax, would become less valuable. A graduated income tax is just according to this decision procedure and the difference principle, because it is the sort of system that would be agreed to, under fair circumstances, by individuals if they had a choice to do so in the historical narrative. It is in my individual self-interest that some people innovate and earn a higher wage, because that higher wage benefits everyone, and in particular those who are most impacted by social programs, such as poor people and other marginalized groups.

Those are distributive principles, focused on how social and economic inequalities should be distributed. There's a separate question not about the distribution of *goods* but instead on the distribution of *rights*. In the state of nature, we had infinite liberties and in the social contract, we sacrificed some of them for self-interest. I agreed not to kill you and steal your cabbage, and you agreed not to kill me and steal my chickens, and we were both better for it. Behind the veil of ignorance, what manner of limitations on our individual freedoms would we agree to on this front? Remember the decision procedure that rejected a principle that would benefit some at the expense of others, and the principle that we endorsed, which said that the system we agree to should include liberties that benefit me; I would never give up any of my individual liberties, except that doing so would have greater benefit to myself. If each person reasoned this way, we would have the greatest number of freedoms possible, so long as the expression of any of those freedoms does not infringe on the freedom of someone else.

---

3. Rawls, *Theory of Justice*, 53.

Consider an alternative decision, in which the parties might have chosen average utility—a structure that guarantees the highest average of utility or benefit across all members. However, under average utility, the rights of some members may be severely restricted for the benefit of the majority. For example, a structure that enslaves some small ethnic minority in service to the majority may indeed maximize average utility, since the benefit to the many is greater than the cost to the few; however, no one would endorse a system that may result in his own enslavement from behind the veil. Rawls argued, therefore, that we would reject average utility in favor of this final principle:

> Each individual should be guaranteed access to the most extensive scheme of liberties available, consistent with a similar set of liberties for others.[4]

Philosophers have historically called this *the harm principle*, and it is sometimes better known colloquially to suggest that my own freedoms end where they begin to infringe upon yours. That is, liberty and freedom is fundamental, and everyone should have as much of it as possible, and the only limit we should place on liberty and freedom and rights, including property rights, involves conflict with the liberty and freedoms and rights of others.

It is worth pausing to notice where we are, and how we got there. If we enumerate the so-called principles of justice, they'll look like this:

1. Each individual should be guaranteed access to the most extensive scheme of liberties available, consistent with a similar set of liberties for others.
2. Social and economic inequalities are just if:
    a. they are attached to office and positions available to everyone;
    b. they are to the benefit of everyone, and in particular the least advantaged members of society.

These are the principles we can use to evaluate the institutions of a society. If the institutions conform to them, then that society, or the institutions that make up that society, and the structure of the society as a whole, are said to be just. And just in case institutions fail to protect or deliver one of these principles, then that is a place where injustice can be located in the structure of that society. And how did we arrive at them? By mimicking a process by which any person, if given the opportunity to agree with them, would agree with them, by assuming that each individual

---

4. Rawls, *Theory of Justice*, 53.

is both self-interested, and free and able to make choices to achieve his own self-interest. So no matter who you are, if you were called upon to create a society that is designed in a way that each person, no matter who they are, would agree to it, a society governed by these principles would do it.

Works Referenced in This Chapter

Rawls, John (1971/1999). *A Theory of Justice.*
Hobbes, Thomas (1651/1994). *Leviathan.*

Further Suggested Readings

Wolff, Robert P. (1973). *In Defense of Anarchism.*

CHAPTER 10

Artificial Intelligence

As is so often the case, the place to begin is to clearly define our terms. So I want to tell you about a theory that philosophers call "functionalism" in order also to clearly define what Searle and Turing are going to call "Strong Artificial Intelligence" (or "Strong AI"). Let us do so by starting with a question: If aliens from outer space exist, and it turns out they have a physiology that is entirely different from the carbon-based physiology that you and I share with most life on earth, *would it be possible for them to feel pain?* The question is not asking you to speculate about whether aliens do feel pain, or will they when we meet them. Rather, it's a conceptual question that asks whether the specifics of our carbon-based nervous systems are necessary for the experience that you and I identify as pain.

Your experience of pain is caused when certain categories of nerves in your central nervous system (CNS)—called "C Fibers"—are damaged or activated, either through trauma or some other means. (C Fibers are activated by capsaicin, which is the ingredient in spicy foods like chili peppers and also pepper spray). C Fibers have other uses, but they're the ones associated with pain in your CNS. Now, space aliens with a different physiology lack these C Fibers. But when the space aliens are burned, stabbed, or crushed, or eat spicy food, they exhibit the same reaction that we would associate with what we experience as pain (they try to avoid the stimulus, they nurse the site of the wound, etc.). Let us say that they even understand and master spoken English, and their description of their experience lines up with what you expect to be the experience of pain. If you judge that what the space aliens are experiencing is pain, then your judgment is that pain is not identical with C Fiber firing, and instead you've adopted what we'll call a "functionalist" attitude toward mental states. Mental states—you can see we're halfway to a discussion about AI already.

So what is functionalism? Some things are defined by what makes them up, such as water. Water = H2O. Anything else in the universe that has all the same properties of water, but isn't strictly defined by the specific chemical constituency of H2O simply is not water. It's something else, no matter how similar, or even exactly similar, to water all of its other properties might be. Water is not defined by its function, but rather by its chemical makeup. Other things, like "flying" are defined entirely by their function. There are many ways to fly. The method of flight achieved by a helicopter is entirely different from the method employed by a rocket, and neither is very similar to what a bumble bee does, or a paper airplane. The concept of "flying" is entirely a functional one and doesn't depend at all on what chemical or physical process is used to achieve it. And if you're like most people, your intuition is probably that mental states are more like the concept of "fly" than they are like "water"; aliens could feel pain even if their physical makeup is dissimilar to humans. If that's right, then mental states are functional states.

Functionalism therefore has a strict and precise definition of a mental state, which we just derived by thinking about pain. According to the functionalist, mental states are defined not in terms of some specific physical makeup, but rather in terms of (1) sensory input, (2) behavioral output, and (3) other mental states. Pain then is caused by a bodily injury (that's the physical input), invokes certain behaviors like wincing or nursing the area (that's the physical output), and finally is associated with distress or desire to reduce or eliminate the pain (that's the mental state). Pain for the functionalist is just anything with the right (1) sensory cause, associated with (2) a behavior, and (3) another mental state.

Now here's where things get interesting. Functionalism has a certain philosophical problem: it appears to be circular. Looking at the definition of mental states generally, and pain in particular, you can see that mental states are defined in terms of mental states—we can't seem to invoke one mental state without evoking another mental state. And that's fine as far as it goes, but it draws the whole concept into question if we're trying to use it as a definition. Definitions usually can't be circular, since relying on the concept to explain the concept risks being trivial and unhelpful. If you don't know what the color blue is, imagine I try to explain by telling you that "blue is the color that all the blue things are." Well, what I've said is technically true, but it's not very useful as a definition, which among other things should be explanatory, and should do so by invoking some other useful concept. "Blue is the color that all the blue things are" is only useful if you already know the color that blue things are, and if you don't, it'll never tell you anything you need to know. It is true but only trivially so.

What does this have to do with artificial intelligence? The functionalist recognizes the inherent circularity of their definition, and they offer as a solution to the problem what we now refer to as a "Turing machine." Let us briefly identify what a Turing machine is and how it works. A Turing machine is a theoretical device, but it can be instantiated in the real world. It is deviously simple, but the concept powers the world that you and I live in. In its original form, as described by Alan Turing, a Turing machine consists of:

1. An infinitely long tape divided into boxes
2. A scanner/printer that can read, erase, and/or write what's in the box
3. A finite set of symbols to write, one per box
4. A finite set of machine states that instruct the scanner/printer what to do when it reads a box

It's as simple as that. At each stage, the scanner reads an input, which consists of some instructions, which the machine carries out, before it returns to a state of waiting for new instructions. As a very simple example, a vending machine that sells soda is a Turing machine. I owe this example to the philosopher Ned Block, from his article, "What Is Functionalism?" (1980). Table 1 displays the machine table for a Coke machine.

Bear with me as I explain how a Coke machine works in excruciating detail. The machine starts in State 1 (S1), and awaits an input. If I input fifty cents, the instructions tell the machine to move to State 2 (S2) and await input. If I input fifty cents again, the machine delivers a Coke, and returns to S1, and awaits input. What happened? I put in fifty cents, then I put in fifty more cents, and I got a Coke. The machine worked! But there's more. Let's start over. The machine starts in S1 and awaits an input. If I put in one dollar, the machine delivers my Coke, and stays in S1, and awaits an input. Great. So far so good, and working as expected. Let's start over one more time. The machine starts in S1 and awaits an input. I put in fifty cents. The machine changes to S2 and awaits an input. What happens if I now put in one dollar? Well, look at the machine table! The instructions tell the machine to deliver my Coke, give me fifty cents change, and return to S1, where it awaits for input.

	State 1 (S1)	State 2 (S2)
Input $.50	- Change to S2	- Deliver Coke - Return to S1
Input $1	- Deliver Coke - Stay in S1	- Deliver Coke - Deliver $.50 - Change to S1

Table 1. Machine state for a vending machine

I apologize for these excruciating details, but thinking about the vending machine as an example, you can probably see that it's just an extremely simplified version of what any digital computer does. The machine on the desk in your office is, for the purposes of this example, simply sitting there waiting for an input from you. When you give it some command, such as "show me the home page for Google," it's literally performing the exact function as described above, just many hundreds of thousands of times per second, with many more than two machine states, and many more than two inputs. However, the main lesson here is that what computers do—and *all* they do—is manipulate symbols, which for a digital computer is just a string of ones and zeros. The choice for the vending machine was binary—dollar or fifty cents—which in the table above we could have easily represented as a choice between a one or a zero. Yes or no, up or down, one or zero, coin or bill: these are all binary choices.

Why are we talking about Turing machines? Turing machines aren't real machines; they're a mathematical abstraction. The vending machine above is not really a Turing machine, but rather a kind of instantiation of one. Alan Turing argued that a sufficiently complex digital computer of the type described above could, at least in principle, have a conversation with a person on any subject, asking and answering questions, according to a certain set of rules and guidelines. And, according to Turing, if that machine were able to fool a human into thinking that he's talking with another person, then there really is no principled way to argue that a person is intelligent and the machine is not. That's the simplified version of the Turing test.

Put the other way, as an answer to the question, "Can a computer think?," Turing suggested what he called the Imitation Game. A simplified version of the game goes like this. Person A is a man, and person B is a woman. Assume that they're in separate rooms, communicating with each other and with person C via a two-way text-based interface. It is the job of person C to determine which of A and B is the man and which is the woman, by asking questions. Person A wants to fool person C, and person B wants to help person C. So for example, person C may ask person A, "How long is your hair," but person A may lie, or give ambiguous answers, such as, "It comes about down to my ears." Person B may say, "I am definitely the woman," but of course, as person B could be the one telling the lie, there is no way for person C to make this distinction. If you were person C, could you solve this game?

The game with persons A, B, and C is an analogy for the Imitation Game. If we were to replace a machine with person A, the question is whether the same would hold. That is, would a machine be able to imitate a person in such a way that by the end of the questioning, person C would believe that he's talking to a person? If so, the machine is said to have passed the test. Notice that this is not quite the same question as "Can a machine think?" Turing himself argued that this question is poorly formed, depends on controversial definitions of the terms "machine" and "think," and lends itself to a popular, rather than a philosophical, resolution. Instead, the question posed by the imitation game is one that can be answered (pretty obviously in the affirmative) and which gives great insight into the future of artificial intelligence.

Let us finish by looking quickly again at the philosophical position we called functionalism. Remember that according to functionalism, the view that a concept such as "intelligent" relies not on the kind of thing it is, but rather the thing's function, or what it does. And remember that we said that functionalism has a circularity problem, meaning that it's difficult to see how one can define mental state without invoking another mental state right in the definition.

Why is circularity a problem? Recall the unhelpful circularity when we define "blue" in terms of "all blue things"; it doesn't tell you anything new, and an understanding of the concept of blue is needed in order to apply the definition in order to understand blue. Cases such as this one are said to be *viciously* circular. But not all circular arguments are vicious in this way. Consider the economist who is explaining why a geographical area is economically depressed, by pointing to the fact that highly skilled workers are leaving the area. But as an explanation for why these workers are leaving, he points to the economic depression of the area. He's explaining the economic depression in terms of lack of workers, but explaining lack of workers in terms of economic depression. And yet, we're able to understand and apply the various parts of this explanation to, for example, consider a solution to this economic problem. Likewise, a doctor may explain that the more insulin a diabetic has in his blood, the more rapidly he will gain weight. And yet, if a diabetic gains weight, he will produce more insulin in the blood. There is no fallacy in either case, and you can see why. In the case of the diabetic and the economist, we're able to understand these two causes in terms of the feedback loop. And further, at least from one point of view, neither feedback loop is vicious, since the man could go on gaining more and more weight, and the geographic area could get more and more economically depressed. And in both cases we can understand why. Unlike in the example of "blue," the explanation is helpful.

As a response to the circularity problem, the functionalist points to the Turing machine, which appears to be able to satisfy the imitation game, while also satisfying the functional requirement of intelligence, being made of something other than a human brain. Importantly, while the functionalist definition of "mental state" requires appeal to another mental state, this is also true of Turing machines themselves. The Turing machine's definition of machine intelligence is also circular, but is satisfactorily explanatory. The functionalist simply embraces the circularity of their definition of mental states.

It doesn't mean we can't understand what those states are, or how they work as a whole. The descriptions of the various machine states provide the full information needed to understand those states. They don't just help you understand the states; they are the full descriptions. There's nothing more to say.

Searle defines strong AI in this way, which he thinks should capture intuitively what we popularly think of AI: "The appropriately programmed computer literally has cognitive states and that the programs thereby explain human cognition. . . . The mind is to the brain as the program is to the computer hardware."[1] The idea here is that there is nothing particularly biological about minds. Yours happens to be biological but a mind doesn't have to be. Instead, any physical thing with the right inputs and outputs would be a mind in exactly the same way that your mind is a mind. This could be made of silicone transistors and wires. Or it could be made of beer cans and windmills. What's important for strong AI is that so long as it has the right program, it would have a mind. Implementing the right program is all that is required for a physical thing to have a mind.

Let's introduce two more piece of vocabulary before we see how Searle's objection works against strong AI: *syntax* and *semantics*.

Syntax is simply all of the *formal* features of some language. Take for example this:

φιλοσοφία

(For this example to work, I assume you don't read any ancient Greek, which is the language that this word is in. If you do, substitute this for a different word in a different language that you don't read). Now, even if you

---

1. Searle, "Minds, Brains, and Programs," 417.

don't read ancient Greek, there's lots you can say about this word. Notice that the third symbol is taller than all the others. Notice that the eighth symbol has a little line over it. Notice that the first symbol and the seventh appear identical. Notice that the spacing in between the various symbols is uniform. Notice that the fourth symbol appears to be a perfect circle, and etc. You don't have to read the language to make many, many more judgments about the *formal* features of that language.

You could do other things with it, too. You could copy/paste it into a Word document. You could transcribe it onto your notebook. You could print it out onto a bumper sticker. I could give you instructions about how to join it up with other words, using other *formal* features of this language (such as, for example, a word that comes before or after this word must be separated by at least one space). In fact, if you had the time and attention, I could give you all kinds of instructions about what other sets of symbols do and don't come after it. You could then spend years writing out the symbols, and then writing out other symbols according to the *formal* syntactic rules that I provide you.

However, one thing you can't learn simply from the *formal* features of the language is the meaning and content of the word. That is, no matter how closely you examine the various *formal* aspects of the language (moving the letters around, studying their height and structure), you can never move from those syntactic elements of the language to understand what that meaning of that particular arrangement of letters represents in that language. And by this, we mean that one cannot ever move from a familiarity with the syntax and structure of a language, to its semantics, which is the meaning and content of the language.

Now remember what a Turing machine is: it's a digital computer. What it does, and all it does, is to read and to write digits according to some algorithm. A digital computer, which reads and writes zeros and ones, is nothing more than a symbol manipulation machine, and it can never move from an understanding of the *formal*, syntactic structure of a language, to an understanding of the semantic meaning and content of the various symbols and words. A machine can never do what your mind does, because human thoughts involve the understanding of the meaning of symbols, which is entirely inaccessible to digital computers. Searle writes:

> This view has the consequence that there is nothing essentially biological about the human mind. The brain just happens to be one of an indefinitely large number of different kinds of hardware computers that could sustain the programs which make up human intelligence. On this view, any physical system whatever

that had the right program with the right inputs and outputs would have a mind in exactly the same sense that you and I have minds. So, for example, if you made a computer out of old beer cans powered by windmills; if it had the right program, it would have to have a mind. And the point is not that for all we know it might have thoughts and feelings, but rather that it must have thoughts and feelings, because that is all there is to having thoughts and feelings: implementing the right program.[2]

Central to Searle's argument is a very famous thought experiment, which has come to be known in philosophy and the study of AI as *The Chinese Room*. Imagine that you, an English speaker, are locked in a small room. In this room is a little window to your left, and another to your right. In front of each window is a little basket, and in front of you is a book, written in English, that tells you how to manipulate Chinese symbols. The book has rules like, "If you get a Chinese symbol in the left basket that looks like a little house with a bird, then put it in the right basket with a Chinese symbol that looks like a pyramid with a tree." Let us call the symbols in the left basket *questions* and the symbols you put in the right basket *answers*.

Imagine further that the rule book contains a very thorough list of instructions for linking questions and answers. In fact, over time, you get so good at your job that your performance in the room is indistinguishable from similar work performed by any native Chinese speaker. You're in your little room, all day, shuffling Chinese symbols around from the left to the right. On the basis of this thought experiment, no matter how long you're in the room, there is no way you could ever learn any Chinese at all, simply by manipulating these formal symbols.

And now, importantly, that's the exact situation that a digital computer is in. We never give them any instructions about how to do anything other than manipulate symbols. By definition, that's not only all we ever tell them, it's all we can ever tell them. Because of the type of thing that they are (viz., symbol manipulators), they can't be given any information about the meaning of the symbols, and so they can never understand language the way people do. Understanding is a mental state that a mere functionally described machine can never have.

> Is instantiating or implementing the right computer program with the right inputs and outputs, sufficient for, or constitutive of, thinking? ... The answer is clearly "no." And it is "no" for the reason that we have spelled out, namely, the computer program is defined purely syntactically. But thinking is more than just a

---

2. Searle, *Mind, Brains, and Science*, 26.

matter of manipulating meaningless symbols, it involves meaningful semantic contents. These semantic contents are what we mean by "meaning."[3]

So if functionalism is just defined in terms of inputs and outputs, then functionalism must be false, because inputs and outputs are just a matter of syntax. And so there is clearly something else that we mean by meaning. Digital computers can *simulate* understanding, just as you in the room may come to *simulate* understanding of the Chinese language. But just as you can never come to understand the meaning of the Chinese symbols just through the act of converting them in the room with the rule book, neither too can a digital computer ever *have* understanding.

Before we close the chapter, let us consider one way to answer Searle's objection to functionalism, and his argument against the possibility of strong AI. This is sometimes called the *systems response*. It goes like this: Let us agree that the person inside the room does not understand Chinese, and given the contours of the example, and the way he interacts with the symbols, he could never come to understand Chinese. But, according to the systems response, this misses the point. According to functionalism and the defenders of strong AI, what Searle misunderstands is that the thing that's understanding Chinese is not the person in the room; what it means to understand Chinese is the entire picture—the person and his book, but also the tiles, the room, the two little windows, and the symbols that come in and the symbols that go out. The system response objects to Searle's thought experiment and argument on the basis that all there is to understanding Chinese is having inputs, taking them in, and giving out the correct outputs. Understood this way, the entire room, including the windows, the baskets, the book, and the tiles, is just a reasonable demonstration of what it means to understand Chinese.

Here is Searle's answer to the systems response. He writes:

> Some people attempt to answer the Chinese room example by saying that the whole system understands Chinese. The idea here is that though I, the person in the room manipulating the symbols do not understand Chinese, I am just the central processing unit of the computer system. They argue that it is the whole system, including the room, the baskets full of symbols and the ledgers containing the programs and perhaps other items as well, taken as a totality, that understands Chinese. But this is subject to exactly the same objection I made before. There is no way that the system can get from the syntax to the

---

3. Searle, *Mind, Brains, and Science*, 34.

semantics. I, as the central processing unit have no way of figuring out what any of these symbols mean; but then neither does the whole system.[4]

I will leave it to you, the reader, to judge whether Searle's answer to the systems response is successful and to decide who you think is right about the possibility of the existence of strong AI. The central argument here is that a digital computer is functionally indistinct from a human brain, and yet we think that a human is able to take away a semantic meaning from symbols that are entirely inaccessible to a machine that only has access to the syntactic content. And yet for the functionalist, this may be largely irrelevant, if we put aside complex philosophical questions of thinking and understanding and merely approach machines, just as we do other people, as agents who exhibit certain behaviors in the face of certain environmental stimuli.

Works Referenced in This Chapter

Searle, John R. (1984) *Minds, Brains and Science.*
Searle, John R. (1980). "Minds, Brains and Programs."
Turing, Alan (1950). "Computing Machinery and Intelligence."
Turing, Alan (1936). "On Computable Numbers, with an Application to the Entscheidungsproblem."
Block, Ned (1980). *Readings in Philosophy of Psychology*, vol. 1.

Further Suggested Reading

DiMatteo, L. A., C. Poncibò, and M. Cannarsa (2022). *The Cambridge Handbook of Artificial Intelligence: Global Perspectives on Law and Ethics.*

---

4. Searle, *Mind, Brains, and Science*, 32.

CHAPTER 11

Paradoxes

A PARADOX IS A case in which there are two choices and neither is a good one. It begins with a reasonable sounding argument, but which then leads to an implausible or seemingly contradictory conclusion. The challenge of a paradox is to find out where we went wrong in our assumptions, or else what went wrong with the logic that led to the conclusion. Obviously, the solution to a paradox is either to give up one or more of the initial reasons that we started with, or else reject the conclusion that seems to follow from them. A paradox is a case where we know that doing one of these things is necessary, but we're reluctant to do either.

Let's start with an easy one. Take a look at the sentence inside of the box in Figure 1, below.

Is it true? Or is it false?

This is known as "the liar's paradox." You can see immediately that it's a paradox if you think about it. The problem is that if what is written in the box is true, then it is false, since what it is truly claiming is that it's false. On the other hand, if it's false, then what it is claiming is that it is false, so it cannot be false, and so it must be true. So if what it says is false, it must be true. And if what it says is true, it must be false. This paradox, which is simple to state, has proved to be one of the more difficult to solve for thousands of years.

> **The Liar's Paradox**
>
> The Sentence in this Box is False.

Figure 1. The Liar's Paradox

Let us put a pin in trying to solve the liar's paradox and think about what makes a paradox. To begin, if we think of a paradox as trying to persuade you of something by giving you reasons to believe it, then it is what we've been calling an argument. An argument, remember, is not just disagreement, and it's not just contradiction. As Graham Chapman stated in a well-known and well-loved sketch by *Monty Python's Flying Circus* (episode 29, 1972), an argument is "a connected series of statements intended to establish a definite proposition. A contradiction is just the automatic gainsaying of anything the other person says." To which, of course, John Cleese replies, that, "no it's not."

But here Cleese, himself a lifelong friend to philosophers, is wrong. All arguments have two parts: the premises and the conclusion that is supported by the premises by reason and logic. All of this is to say that a paradox is just a kind of argument that goes wrong somehow. And by looking at what an argument is, there are only three places is can go wrong: the conclusion, the premises, or the reasoning. Finally, here's a definition of a paradox, which I owe to R. M. Sainsbury from his little book *Paradoxes*: a paradox is an apparently unacceptable conclusion, derived from apparently acceptable premises, using apparently acceptable reasoning or logic. Thus, the solution to a paradox is equally as straightforward: we either deny the strength of the logic, deny the truth of the assumptions or premises, or we deny that the conclusion follows from them. The difficulty is, of course, knowing which to deny. Paradoxes come on a spectrum from easy to solve to very difficult to solve. The liar's paradox turns out, as we noted, to be quite difficult to solve. What follows—call it the "barber paradox"—is an example a solution that is a bit simpler.

There is apparently a barber who lives in the remote mountains of Sicily, and this barber is known to shave all and only those who do not shave themselves. Does the barber shave himself? Well, if the barber is a person who does shave himself, then since the barber shaves all and only those who do not shave themselves, then he does not shave himself. On the other hand, if he does not shave himself, then he does shave himself, because of course, he does shave all of those who do not shave themselves. So if he does shave himself then he doesn't, and if he doesn't, then he does. It's a paradox.

The template for solving a paradox, remember, is to deny the assumption, deny the reasoning, or deny that the conclusion follows. Once we see what the conclusions are, and how they are derived, it is also easy to see that what must be rejected is the initial assumption—i.e., there is no such person, hidden though he may be in more Sicilian mountains, who shaves all and only people who do not shave themselves. By denying the initial assumption, we come to a resolution about the impossibility of the paradox itself.

While this resolution is somewhat satisfying, solutions of this sort are frequently unavailable to us, as you can see in, for example, the liar's paradox. We cannot simply deny that there is a sentence inside of the box in Figure 1. Can we?

The liar's paradox and the barber's paradox are a category of paradoxes that we can call "self-referential": the strength of the paradox owes at least in part to the fact that it is referring to itself. But of course not all self-referential sentences are paradoxical. Indeed, this very sentence is self-referential, and it involves no paradox at all. And not all paradoxes are self-referential, as we will see.

It is easy to think of paradoxes as party tricks or logic games; fun to state, fun to try to solve, but otherwise of very little actual value. But I think this is a mistake. In the history of ideas, paradoxes have pointed to serious deficits in commonly accepted positions, and engaging with these ideas seriously has led to notable advances in the sciences and humanities. In all cases, to wrestle with a paradox is to risk wading into deep waters, and in some cases, their solution points to an important revolution of thought.

One important example is due to Bertrand Russell, the twentieth-century philosopher who we met in chapter 1. In the nineteenth and twentieth centuries, there was an interest among mathematicians in identifying the logical and epistemological grounding for mathematics and arithmetic. Even in its simplest terms, how do you know that 1+1=2? It's because every time you or anyone else has put one thing next to another thing, you've had two things. But as we know from chapter 3, this is an inductive generalization, and we know that the problem of induction shows that no matter how many experiences of some type of phenomenon you have, such as having two things when you put one thing next to another thing, it is possible that your conclusion doesn't follow from your premises. Just as it's hard to see how the sun could rise in the west, or a fire wouldn't burn you, it's hard to see how putting one thing next to another thing could mean having three things. It's extremely unlikely, but it's not logically impossible, if the basis on which we believe it is an inductive one. Is there a stronger, necessary foundation on which we can build mathematics?

Gottlob Frege, the German mathematician and father of analytic philosophy, set out to provide that groundwork in a field called *set theory*. I'll try to simplify the attempted solution, since the deep mathematical problem is not what's important here. We know that Socrates is a man, meaning that he's a member of the class or *set* of men. If he's a member of the set of men then he's a man. Can sets be members of sets? Yes. The set of all men is a member of the set of sets with more than 100 members. If you think about "the set of all sets with more than 100 members," then there are lots of members of that set, such as the set of all the grains of sand on Spanish beaches, or the set of all books currently held in the British Library. And some things are not members of that set, such as the set of all people who have been the American president (as of 2024 the set has forty-five members). So the set of all people who have been American president is not a member of the set of sets with more than 100 members.

Some sets are members of themselves; the set of all sets is also a set, and so is a member of itself. Also you can see that the set of all sets with more than 100 members is also a member of itself, since it has more than 100 members. But most sets are not members of themselves; the set of all men is not a man, and the set of all people who were once president of the United States was never itself the president (it never will be, since the US Constitution prohibits sets from serving as president).

Now think about this one: The set of all sets that are not members of themselves. Is it a member of itself? Well, if it is a member of itself, then it is itself a set that is not a member of itself. But that can't be, because it is a member of itself. But if it is not a member of itself, then it is, because it would be a set that is not a member of itself. You can see that if it is, then it cannot be, but if it's not, then it is. It's a paradox.

Russell described this paradox to demonstrate a deep systematic problem with Frege's project of mathematical foundations. I introduce Russell's paradox to you for two reasons. First, it's a self-referential paradox in the same way that the liar's paradox and the barber's paradox are. But second, Russell's paradox was wildly important for exposing a defect in the foundational reasoning that was meant to provide a groundwork for our reliance on mathematics itself. It showed the failure of the project that Frege and others were engaged in, and introduced the need for a new kind of mathematics. Statistically speaking, you're not a mathematician, so the deep problem that it uncovers, and the enormous amount of work that went into overcoming it, is not what you should necessarily take away. If you're willing to take Russell's and Frege's word for it, then the lesson of this, like so many other paradoxes, is that they're often more than just party games and logic puzzles; instead, they frequently introduce and point to serious and important problems in logic, science, and language.

As I mentioned above, not all paradoxes are self-referential. There is a category of paradox that is just as old as the liar's paradox, but which is not self-referential, and these are known as Zeno's paradoxes, named after the pre-Socratic Greek philosopher. Zeno's paradoxes are typically related to the impossibility of dividing time, space, or movement into parts. Let's look at two such examples and think about how they pointed to problems in the way that people used to understand time, space, and motion, and how updated ways of thinking about those concepts points to a potential solution to the problem.

The first is Zeno's *arrow paradox* (which is somewhat different from other arrow paradoxes with which some readers may be familiar). It's pretty easy to see how the paradox works. Consider an arrow which has left the bow, but before hitting its target. Zeno argues that in each stage in its flight it is in a "now," by which he means that at each stage of its flight the arrow takes up a particular space in time. Since time is composed of moments, and at each of these moments the arrow fully takes up some space (in that particular moment it's not in two places), then it must be at rest. But if at each and every time the arrow is in a "now," then the flying arrow is motionless in each "now." Since at every instant the arrow is at some position, then at each of those instants the arrow is motionless. But if it is motionless at each instant, and time is composed of many instants, then motion is impossible. It would seem that an arrow shot from a bow cannot possibly fly through the air as it is constantly at rest.

While the arrow paradox involves the infinite division of time, the next puzzle, Zeno's paradox of Achilles and the tortoise, involves the concept that space can be divided infinitely.

Achilles and a tortoise are in a foot race of 200 meters. Because Achilles is so swift of foot, he gives the tortoise a 100 meter head start. However, in doing so, Achilles can never catch the tortoise. To see why, assume that they both run at a constant speed, though of course Achilles's pace will be ten times faster than the tortoise's pace. After some time, Achilles will have run 100 meters, but during that time, the tortoise will also have moved forward 10 meters. Very quickly Achilles will close that distance by advancing to 110 meters, but during that time, the tortoise will have moved ahead one meter. If we keep going, Achilles will advance to the 111 meter mark, but by then, the tortoise will have moved ahead one tenth of a meter. Even though Achilles can then quickly cover that space, the tortoise will again move ahead. Whenever Achilles arrives to a point where the tortoise has been, because space is infinitely divisible there is still some distance he must travel before he can reach the tortoise. And so no matter the speed of either, or the total distance of the race, with a head start of any length the faster runner can never overtake the slower one.

With regard to the arrow paradox, there is a standard way to resolve the paradox, and a more interesting one. To see how the standard answer works, just remember the scientific definition of "distance":

$D = V \times T$

This just means that distance equals velocity multiplied by time. When we pick a moment (a "now") to observe the arrow, how much time are we giving it when we say "it's here now"? If velocity is just the rate of change, then it shouldn't be surprising that if we give the arrow zero time to move, then also the distance traveled would also be zero. The number on the left of the equals sign would be zero because one of the numbers on the right is zero. Zeno is just pulling a fast one on us. Looking at that simple equation, if time is zero and distance is zero, then what's velocity? It could be anything at all. It could be some huge number. It certainly doesn't follow, as Zeno suggests, that it must also be zero.

There is a more sophisticated way to think about the arrow paradox, but it helps to see first the solution to Achilles and the tortoise. A paradox is a valuable thing because it forces us to think more clearly about something we were not already clear about, or didn't realize we were unclear about. It draws unclarity into focus. And often, a paradox means giving up something that we might have assumed—knowingly or not—to be true. Zeno is not really showing us that Achilles can't catch the tortoise; of course Achilles can catch a tortoise. He's actually showing us something else.

The paradox of Achilles and the tortoise turns on the infinite divisibility of space. It's true that there's no last instant at which Achilles fails to catch the tortoise. That's the epistemological price we pay: there are an infinite number of instances at which he fails to overtake the tortoise. What the story shows is that there are an infinite number of instances, or sequence of events, in which he fails to draw even with the tortoise. But what it doesn't show is that there isn't a first instant in which he does draw even with the tortoise. And that's the resolution. Zeno is hoping that we're confused about these two distinct facts and infer that, since there's no last instant in which he fails to catch the tortoise, that there is also no first instant in which he does overtake the tortoise. The fallacy occurs because Zeno hopes that you don't notice that even though there's no final instance in which he fails to overtake the tortoise, this is not the same as showing that there's no first instance in which he succeeds in overtaking the tortoise.

You're not alone if it takes you a few minutes to see the difference between these two cases, or why one doesn't follow from the other, or why the fallacy of thinking that they're identical leads to the apparent paradox. But if so, don't be embarrassed. If you take a few quiet minutes to give it a think, then we can just add you to the ranks of philosophers who have struggled with these and similar puzzles for thousands of years. Philosophy is the practice of taking the necessary time to think very carefully about complicated problems.

With this answer in place, there is a somewhat more interesting resolution to the arrow paradox that mirrors the paradox of Achilles and the tortoise. Remember that the arrow is at all times somewhere. For simplicity, let's say that the arrow is "here" right "now." Zeno argues that it's kind of stuck in *this* now, and it therefore can't get to the *next* now, and that's why it can't move. But in reality, there is no particular *next* now, because the number of nows in any given time is infinite. You can try it yourself: How many nows, or instants of time, are there in one second? Obviously, you can divide a second in half, and then half again and again. Any interval of time can be divided into an infinite number of instances between any two instants of time. There are always an infinite number of instants, and so there is no *next* now for the arrow to get to.

Just as there's no final moment before Achilles overtakes the tortoise, there's no particular next now to which the arrow can get. But it doesn't follow from there that the arrow cannot get to another now. That's the epistemological price you pay.

Philosophers have been playing the game of paradox for about as long as there have been philosophers, so there are any number of paradoxes for you to struggle with, corresponding to nearly every field of human endeavor. The very existence of paradoxes that exist in the realm of the sciences and humanities points to places where discovery and clarity exist to be discovered.

Works Referenced in This Chapter

Whitehead, Alfred N., and Bertrand Russell (1903). *Principia Mathematica*, vol. 2.
Frege, Gottlob (1879). *Begriffsschrift, a Formula Language, Modeled Upon That of Arithmetic, for Pure Thought*.
Sainsbury, Richard M. (2009). *Paradoxes*.

Further Suggested Reading

Russell, Bertrand (2015). *The Collected Papers of Bertrand Russell.* Vol. 5, *Toward Principia Mathematica, 1905–8.*
Smullyan, Raymond (1986). *This Book Needs No Title: A Budget of Living Paradoxes.*

Bibliography

Anselm. *Proslogion: With the Replies of Gaunilo and Anselm.* Translated by Thomas Williams. Indianapolis: Hackett, 2001 (1078).
Armstrong, David. *What Is a Law of Nature?* Cambridge Philosophy Classics. Cambridge: Cambridge University Press, 2016.
Berkeley, George W. *A Treatise Concerning the Principles of Human Knowledge.* New York: Penguin Classics, 1988.
Blackburn, Simon. *Think: A Compelling Introduction to Philosophy.* Oxford: Oxford University Press, 1999.
Block, Ned. *Readings in Philosophy of Psychology.* Vol. 1. Cambridge: Harvard University Press, 1980.
Boswell, James. *The Life of Samuel Johnson.* Edinburgh: William P. Nimmo, 1873.
Dawkins, Richard. *The Selfish Gene.* Oxford: Oxford University Press, 2017.
Descartes, René. *Discourse on Method and Meditations on First Philosophy.* Translated by Donald A. Cress. 4th ed. Indianapolis: Hackett, 1999 (1641).
DiMatteo, L. A., C. Poncibò, and M. Cannarsa, eds. *The Cambridge Handbook of Artificial Intelligence: Global Perspectives on Law and Ethics.* Cambridge: Cambridge University Press, 2022.
Durant, William. *The Story of Philosophy.* Garden City, NY: Courier Dover, 1926.
Frege, Gottlob. *Begriffsschrift, a Formula Language, Modeled Upon That of Arithmetic, for Pure Thought.* N.p.: Lubrecht & Cramer, 1879.
Herodotus. *Histories Book VIII.* Edited by A. M. Bowie. Cambridge: Cambridge University Press, 1999 (430 BCE).
Hobbes, Thomas. *Leviathan.* Edited by Edwin Curley. Indianapolis: Hackett, 1994 (1651).
Hume, David. *An Inquiry Concerning Human Understanding.* Edited by Eric Steinberg. 2nd ed. Indianapolis: Hackett, 1993 (1748).
———. *Dialogues Concerning Natural Religion.* Edinburgh: William Blackwood, 1907 (1779).
———. *A Treatise of Human Nature.* Oxford: Clarendon, 2011 (1739).
Kant, Immanuel. *Critique of Pure Reason.* Edited and translated by Marcus Weigelt. New York: Penguin, 2007 (1781).
———. *Groundwork for the Metaphysics of Morals.* Edited by Allen W. Wood. New Haven: Yale University Press, 2018 (1785).

Locke, John. *An Essay Concerning Human Understanding*. Philadelphia: Kay & Troutman, 1690.

Midgley, Mary. *Trying Out One's New Sword*. New York: St. Martin's, 1981.

Mill, John S. *Utilitarianism, Liberty & Representative Government*. Rockville, MD: Wildside, 2007 (1863).

Paley, William. *Natural Theology: or, Evidences of the Existence and Attributes of the Deity, Collected from the Appearances of Nature*. Boston: Lincoln and Edmands, 1829.

Plato. *The Trial and Death of Socrates Euthyphro, Apology, Crito, Phaedo*. Indianapolis: Hackett, 1963.

———. *The Republic*. Indianapolis: Hackett, 2004 (375 BCE).

Popper, Karl. *Conjectures and Refutations: The Growth of Scientific Knowledge*. London: Routledge, 1963.

Rachels, James, and Stuart Rachels. *The Elements of Moral Philosophy*. New York: McGraw-Hill, 1986.

Rawls, John. *A Theory of Justice*. Cambridge: Harvard University Press, MA, 1999.

Ruse, Michael. *On Purpose*. Princeton: Princeton University Press, 2017.

Russell, Bertrand. *The Collected Papers of Bertrand Russell*. Vol. 5, *Toward Principia Mathematica, 1905–8*. Edited by Gregory E. Moore. London: Routledge, 2015.

———. *The Problems of Philosophy*. Oxford: Oxford University Press, 1997 (1912).

Sainsbury, Richard M. *Paradoxes*. 3rd ed. Cambridge: Cambridge University Press, 2009.

Searle, John R. *Minds, Brains and Science*. Cambridge: Harvard University Press, 1984.

———. "Minds, Brains, and Programs." *Behavioral and Brain Sciences* 3.3 (1980) 417–57.

Shorto, Robert. *Descartes' Bones: A Skeletal History of the Conflict Between Faith and Reason*. New York: Vintage, 2009.

Smullyan, Raymond. *This Book Needs No Title: A Budget of Living Paradoxes*. New York: Simon and Schuster, 1986.

Turing, Alan. "Computing Machinery and Intelligence." *Mind* 59 (1950) 433–60.

———. "On Computable Numbers, with an Application to the Entscheidungsproblem." *J. of Math* 58 (1936) 345–63.

US Reports. *Schenck v. United States*, 249 US 47. 1918. Periodical.

Whitehead, Alfred N., and Bertrand Russell. *Principia Mathematica*. Vol. 2. Cambridge: Cambridge University Press, 1903.

Wolff, Robert P. *In Defense of Anarchism*. Oakland: University of California Press, 1973.

Index

"1+1=2", 100

abduction, 62
Achilles, 102
Allegory of the Cave, 5–6
altruism, 79, 82
ambiguity, 50
Anselm, Saint of Canterbury, 15, 49–55
Apology, The (Plato), 27
a posteriori, 19
a priori, 19, 49
argument by analogy, 58–60
　　criteria for analyzing, 59–60
argument clinic, 99
argument from design (for the existence of God), 48, 56
argument from ignorance, 36
argument from perceptual relativity, the, 70
Aristotle, 13
arrow paradox, 102
artificial intelligence, 88–97
　　Strong AI, 88
atheism (Berkeley), 75–76

barber paradox, 99
Bentham, Jeremy, 42
Berkeley, George, 67
Blind Watchmaker, The (Dawkins), 62
Boswell, James, 76
brain in a vat, 14

cabbage (soup), 80
Callatians, 37
capital punishment, 3–5
Cartesian skepticism, 10–16
categorical imperative, 44
causation, 21
C Fibers, 88
Chapman, Graham, 99
chicken (soup), 80
Chinese Room (thought experiment), 95–97
circularity, 92
Cleese, John, 99
consequentialism, 42
constant conjunction, 22
creationism, 64

Darwin, Charles 62
Dawkins, Richard, 62
deontology, 43
Descartes, René, 67, 71, 74
descent with ,odification, 63
Dialogues Concerning Natural Religion (Hume), 61
difference principle, 85
disjunction, 29
distance, 103
divine command theory, defined, 27
doubt, hyperbolic, 16
drom-drom, 54–55
Dumbo, 28

egoism, 40
    ethical, 40
    psychological, 40
Einstein, Albert, 8, 19
elephant, 28
Empire State Building, 4
ethical egoism. *See* egoism, ethical.
ethics
    defined, 33
    relationship with religion, 26
Euthyphro dilemma, 26–32
evil demon. *See* evil genius
evil genius, 14
"existence is not a predicate" (for ontological argument), 54–55
"exists" (for ontological argument), 50
eye, 57

falsibiability, 24
fire, yelling in a crowded theater, 59
flying (functionalism), 89
Frege, Gottlob, 101
functionalism, 88

Galileo Galilei, 6, 8, 58, 72
Gaunilo of Marmoutiers, 53
giraffe, 63
Glaucon, 39
God, definition (for ontological argument), 49
greatest island objection (Gaunilo), 53
Greeks, 37

harm principle, 86
Herodotus, 37
Hobbes, Thomas, 79
Holmes, Oliver Wendell, 59
Hume, David, 11, 17, 61
hypothetical imperative, 45

idealism (argument against the existence of the physical world), 65–77
idealism, defined, 65
ideas, 69
inductive generalization, 19

inference to the best explanation. *See* abduction.
infinite divisibility of space, 103
intelligence (functionalism), 92
interaction of minds and bodies, 74
"I think, therefore I am", 15

Johnson, Samuel, 76

Kant, Immanuel, 15, 43, 54
Kierkegaard, Søren, 47

Leaning Tower of Pisa, 73
Lex Luthor, 43
liar's paradox, 98–99
libertarianism, 78
Lincoln, Abraham, 58
Locke, John, 8, 68, 79
logic, 17
    deductive, 17
    formal, 17
logos, 56

matters of fact, 19, 21
Meditations on First Philosophy (Descartes), 11
mens rea. *See* retributivist theory of punishment.
Midgley, Mary, 46
million monkeys (typing on a million typewriters for a million years), 63
Mill, John Stuart, 42
mode (of minds), 71
Monty Python's Flying Circus, 99
moral progress, 37

omnibenevlent, 30
omnipotent, 29
On the Origin of Species (Darwin), 62
ontological argument (for the existence of God), 47–55
ontology, 49
operations of the mind, 68
Oracle of Delphi, 27

Index

Paley, William, 48, 57
paradox, 9, 55
   defined, 98
   of achilles and the tortoise, 102–3
   self-referential, 100
philosophy, defined, 1–7
piety, 28
Plato, 13
Popper, Karl, 19, 23
primary qualities. *See* qualities
principle of fair equality of opportunity, 84
principles of justice, 86
problem of induction, 22, 17–25
Proslogion (Anselm), 49
psychological egoism. *See* egoism.

qualities, 69

Rachels, James, 37
Rawls, John, 79, 81
reductio ad absurdum, 8–9, 53, 55
relations of ideas, 18, 22
relativism, 34
   cultural, 34
   subjective, 34
Republic (Plato), 39
retributivist theory of punishment, 5
ring of Gyges, 39
Rousseau, Jean-Jacques, 79
Ruse, Michael, 64
Russell, Bertrand, 100
Russell's paradox, 101

Sainsbury, R.M., 99
Schenck v. United States (1919), 59
Searle, John, 88, 94
secondary qualities. *See* qualities
semantics, 93

set theory, 101
skepticism
   colloquial, 10
   philosophical, 10
   radical, 67, 75
Smullyan, Raymond, 105
social contract theory, 78–87
Socrates, 33
Socratic Method, 7, 26
state of nature, 81
substratum, 71
swinish objection (to utilitarianism), 43
syllogism, 18
syntax, 93
systems response, 96

teleological argument (for the existence of God), 56–64
teleology, defined, 56
telescope, 58
tortoise, 102
trolley problem, 41
Turing, Alan, 88
Turing machine, 90

unicorn, 49

veil of ignorance, 83
velocity, 103
vending machine, 90–91

watchmaker analogy, 57
water (functionalism), 89
wax, 68
Weasel Program, The, 63
Woff, Robert, 87

Zeno, 102
Zeno's paradoxes, 102

www.ingramcontent.com/pod-product-compliance
Lightning Source LLC
Chambersburg PA
CBHW032234080426

42735CB00008B/850